D0268313

Frances Cole is a GP and Cognitive Behavioral Therapist. In 1996 she developed a primary care-run pain rehabilitation programme and continues to develop her interest in chronic pain management.

Helen Macdonald is a Cognitive Behavioral Psychotherapist and university lecturer specializing in pain management. She has obtained a Master's degree in Cognitive-Behavioral Psychotherapy, with a dissertation examining the effectiveness of assisted self-help for chronic pain. She was recognized as a Chartered Health Psychologist in 2004.

Catherine Carus is a registered Physiotherapist and university lecturer currently teaching at the University of Bradford, she specializes in the assessment and management of musculoskeletal conditions.

Hazel Howden-Leach is a Consultant Academic Developer, working in the UK and Africa. Her expertize lies in designing health-related educational materials and programmes.

The aim of the **Overcoming** series is to enable people with a range of common problems and disorders to take control of their own recovery program. Each title, with its specially tailored programs, is devised by a practising clinician using the latest techniques of cognitive behavioral therapy – techniques which have been shown to be highly effective in changing the way patients think about themselves and their difficulties. The series was initiated in 1993 by Peter Cooper, Professor of Psychology at Reading University and Research Fellow at the University of Cambridge in the UK, whose original volume on overcoming bulimia nervosa and binge-eating continues to help many people in the UK, the USA, Australia and Europe.

Other titles in the series include:

OVERCOMING ANGER AND IRRITABILITY
OVERCOMING ANOREXIA NERVOSA
OVERCOMING ANXIETY
OVERCOMING BODY IMAGE PROBLEMS
OVERCOMING BULIMIA NERVOSA AND BINGE-EATING
OVERCOMING CHILDHOOD TRAUMA
OVERCOMING CHRONIC FATIGUE
OVERCOMING COMPULSIVE GAMBLING
OVERCOMING DEPERSONALIZATON AND FEELINGS OF UNREALITY
OVERCOMING DEPRESSION
OVERCOMING GRIEF
OVERCOMING HEALTH ANXIETY
OVERCOMING LOW SELF-ESTEEM
OVERCOMING MOOD SWINGS
OVERCOMING OBSESSIVE COMPULSIVE DISORDER
OVERCOMING PANIC AND AGRAPHOBIA
OVERCOMING PARANOID AND SUSPICIOUS THOUGHTS
OVERCOMING PROBLEM DRINKING
OVERCOMING RELATIONSHIP PROBLEMS
OVERCOMING SEXUAL PROBLEMS
OVERCOMING SOCIAL ANXIETY AND SHYNESS
OVERCOMING STRESS
OVERCOMING TRAUMATIC STRESS
OVERCOMING WEIGHT PROBLEMS
OVERCOMING WORRY
OVERCOMING YOUR CHILD'S FEARS AND WORRIES
OVERCOMING YOUR CHILD'S SHYNESS AND SOCIAL ANXIETY
OVERCOMING YOUR SMOKING HABIT

All titles in the series are available by mail order.
Please see the order form at the back of this book.
www.overcoming.co.uk

OVERCOMING CHRONIC PAIN

*A self-help manual using
Cognitive Behavioral Techniques*

FRANCES COLE,
HELEN MACDONALD,
CATHERINE CARUS and
HAZEL HOWDEN-LEACH

ROBINSON
London

Constable & Robinson Ltd
3 The Lanchesters
162 Fulham Palace Road
London W6 9ER
www.constablerobinson.com

First published in the UK by Robinson,
an imprint of Constable & Robinson Ltd, 2005, 2010

This edition published in 2010

Copyright © 2005, 2010

The right of Frances Cole, Helen Macdonald, Catherine Carus and Hazel
Howden-Leach to be identified as the author of this work has been asserted by
him in accordance with the Copyright, Designs and Patents Act 1988.

All rights reserved. This book is sold subject to the condition
that it shall not, by way of trade or otherwise, be lent, re-sold,
hired out or otherwise circulated in any form of binding or cover
other than that in which it is published and without a similar condition
including this condition being imposed on the subsequent purchaser.

A copy of the British Library Cataloguing in
Publication data is available from the British Library

Important Note
This book is not intended as a substitute for medical advice or treatment.
Any person with a condition requiring medical attention should consult a
qualified medical practitioner or suitable therapist.

ISBN: 978-1-84119-970-2

LANCASHIRE COUNTY LIBRARY	
3011812693280 9	
Askews & Holts	08-May-2013
616.0472 COL	£10.99
NCA	

Table of contents

Acknowledgements

Many individuals and teams have given us invaluable advice, feedback and support during the preparation of this book, for which we are deeply grateful. We would specifically like to thank Chris Williams, Christine Padesky, Karina Lovell, Glenda Wallace and Paul Gilbert for allowing us to use their materials, models and prior experience.

We would not have been able to prepare this without the input of:

The Mexborough Montagu Hospital Pain Management Team, Doncaster and Bassetlaw NHS Trust, South Yorkshire.

The Pain Rehabilitation Programme, Pain Clinic and Clinical Psychology Departments at Bradford NHS Teaching Hospitals Trust, Bradford.

Gill Fletcher, Tracy Sanderson and Anne Hesselden, Bradford and Huddersfield physiotherapy colleagues for being most supportive.

Patients and staff in primary care in Bradford and Huddersfield GP practices.

Pete Moore, Expert Patient Programme Trainer for advice and support.

Academic encouragement, clinical supervision and constructive comments from Anni Telford and the staff at the University of Derby Unit for Psychotherapeutic Practice and Research, Tom Ricketts, Penny Stevens, and Judith Hooper, Director of Public Health, North Kirklees PCT who helped in the final stages and colleagues from the Division of Rehabilitation Studies, University of Bradford.

It would not have been possible to complete this without the personal support and tolerance of family and friends; and we would like to thank Doug, Joe, Kiefer, Max and Logan.

Feedback from Shirley Douglas, Sharon Stephenson, Mavis Aitchison, Margaret Hornsby, Peter Norcliffe, Kate Cole and Cate Clark at different stages of the book was so helpful.

Most of all, we are grateful to the pain survivors who used the original workbook materials as they were developed over the last five years. They shared their experiences and gave us feed-back that enabled this book to be brought to its current form.

Frances Cole
Helen Macdonald
Catherine Carus
January 2005

Foreword

People usually try to avoid pain. Sufferers of chronic pain cannot avoid their pain. Fortunately, *Overcoming Chronic Pain* teaches skills that turn pain sufferers into pain managers. By tuning into pain rather than trying to avoid it, sufferers learn to understand personal pain patterns. Understanding pain is the first step towards pain relief. This welcome relief comes about when readers learn a variety of pain management skills taught here in simple, straightforward steps.

This book combines the collective knowledge and wisdom of three pain specialists – Frances Cole (a GP who is also a Cognitive Behavioral Psychotherapist), Helen Macdonald (a Cognitive Behavioral Psychotherapist and mental health nurse) and Catherine Carus (a Physiotherapist) – working as a team with a Learning Technology Adviser, Hazel Howden-Leach. Drawing on feedback from hundreds of pain patients, the authors show readers how to chart a personalized pain model and choose skills to help manage the worst aspects of pain. Over time, readers who practise these skills can become more relaxed, physically fitter, and develop better problem-solving strategies. In addition, chapters teach how to reduce depression, anxiety, anger and the sleep difficulties that often accompany pain.

The biggest challenge to readers of self-help books is to practise the skills taught. No matter how helpful, any book that sits on a shelf offers little benefit. For this reason, chapters in this book are brief. Even a 10-minute read can lead to helpful knowledge. Most of the exercises taught can be learned quickly and practised in 10- or 15-minute segments. Readers can pace themselves and use this book in whatever timeframe fits each day's planning.

Chronic pain sufferers are often unaware of the progress in pain management achieved over the past few decades. Even some healthcare providers will not be aware of all the information in this book. *Overcoming Chronic Pain* gives an overview of the most up-to-date techniques. It emphasizes ideas and skills that have been validated by research and successfully used by many pain sufferers.

For example, mood management chapters draw on ideas from Cognitive Behavioral Therapy, a form of psychotherapy that research shows is highly effective for depression and anxiety. The chapter on sleep teaches the research-based practice of 'good sleep hygiene'. The chapter on 'Getting Fitter and Being More Active' combines fitness principles with research on pain. So readers of *Overcoming Chronic Pain* can feel secure that the ideas contained within this book are not simply the opinions of these authors. They are summaries of the best information and practice currently available to understand and manage chronic pain.

Chronic pain can affect every aspect of one's life. No single skill is likely to be sufficient to manage this type of pain. The good news is that groups of skills are highly effective in managing chronic pain. This book teaches you how to choose and learn the skills that are best to cope with life with your pain. As you develop your skills, you can measure your progress, and see positive changes in your confidence, and your daily and social activities. At first, the changes achieved may seem small. But those who stick with a programme can move mountains of distress due to pain. I join the authors in wishing you every success in building your own effective pain management programme.

Christine A. Padesky, Ph.D.
Co-author, *Mind Over Mood: Change How You Feel by Changing the Way You Think*

Introduction
by Peter Cooper

Why cognitive behavioral?

You may have picked up this book uncertain as to why a psychological therapy such as cognitive behavioral and systemic therapy could help you overcome your chronic pain. The first of the two components, cognitive behavior therapy (CBT) was developed initially for the treatment of depression, and the techniques this therapy uses have been found to be extremely effective for a wide range of problems, including compulsive gambling and drug and alcohol addiction. So what is CBT and how does it work?

In the 1950s and 1960s a set of techniques was developed, collectively termed 'behavior therapy'. These techniques shared two basic features. First, they aimed to remove symptoms (such as anxiety) by dealing with those symptoms themselves, rather than their deep-seated underlying historical causes (traditionally the focus of psychoanalysis, the approach developed by Sigmund Freud and his followers). Second, they were techniques loosely related to what laboratory psychologists were finding out about the mechanisms of learning, which could potentially be put to the test, or had already been proven to be of practical value to sufferers. The area where these techniques proved to be of most value was in the treatment of anxiety disorders, especially specific phobias (such as fear of animals or heights) and agoraphobia, both notoriously difficult to treat using conventional psychotherapies.

After an initial flush of enthusiasm, discontent with behavior therapy grew. There were a number of reasons for this, an important one of which was the fact that behavior therapy did not deal with the internal thoughts which were so obviously central to the distress that patients were experiencing. In particular, behavior therapy proved inadequate when it came to the treatment of depression. In the late 1960s and early 1970s a treatment was developed for depression called 'cognitive therapy'. The pioneer in this enterprise was an American psychiatrist, Professor Aaron T. Beck, who developed a theory of depression which emphasized the importance of people's depressed styles of thinking. He also specified a new form of therapy. It would not be an exaggeration to say that Beck's work has changed the nature of psychotherapy, not just for depression but for a range of psychological problems.

The techniques introduced by Beck have been merged with the techniques developed earlier by the behavior therapists to produce a therapeutic approach which has come to be known as 'cognitive behavioral therapy'. This therapy has been subjected to the strictest scientific testing and it has been found to be a highly successful treatment for a significant proportion of cases of depression. It has now become clear that specific patterns of thinking identified by Beck are associated with a wide range of psychological problems and that the treatments which deal with these styles of thinking are highly effective. So, effective cognitive behavioral treatments have been developed for anxiety disorders, like panic disorder, generalized anxiety disorder, specific phobias and social phobia, obsessive compulsive disorders, and hypochondriasis (health anxiety), as well as for other conditions such as compulsive gambling, alcohol and drug addiction, and eating disorders like bulimia nervosa and binge-eating disorder. Indeed, cognitive behavioral techniques have a wide application beyond the narrow categories of psychological disorders: they have been applied effectively, for example, to helping people with low self-esteem, those with marital difficulties or weight problems, those who wish to give up smoking, and, as in this book, those living with chronic pain.

The starting-point for CBT is that the way we think, feel and behave are all intimately linked, and changing the way we think about ourselves, our experiences and the world around us changes the way we feel and what we are able to do. So, by helping a depressed person identify and challenge their automatic depressive thoughts, a route out of the cycle of depressive thoughts and feelings can be found. Similarly, habitual responses are driven by a nexus of thoughts, feelings and behavior; and CBT, as you will discover from this book, by providing a means for the behavior to he brought under cognitive control, enables these responses to be undermined and a different kind of life to be possible.

Although effective CBT treatments have been developed for a wide range of problems, they are not widely available, and when people try to help themselves they often make matters worse. In recent years the community of cognitive behavioral therapists has responded to this situation. What they have done is to take the principles and techniques of specific cognitive behavioral therapies for particular problems and present them in self-help manuals. These manuals specify a systematic programme of treatment which the individual sufferer is advised to work through to overcome their difficulties. In this way, cognitive behavioral therapeutic techniques of proven value are being made available on the widest possible basis.

Self-help manuals are never going to replace therapists. Many people will need individual treatment from a qualified therapist. It is also the case that, despite the widespread success of cognitive behavioral therapy, some people will not respond to it and will need one of the other treatments available. Nevertheless, although research on the use of these self-help manuals is at an early stage, the work done to date indicates that for a great many people such a manual will prove sufficient for them to overcome their problems without professional help.

Many people suffer silently and secretly for years. Sometimes appropriate help is not forthcoming despite their efforts to find it. Sometimes they feel too ashamed or guilty to reveal their problems to anyone. For many of these people the cognitive behavioral self-help manual will provide a lifeline to recovery and a better future.

Professor Peter Cooper
The University of Reading, 2005

Introduction

This book is designed to help you manage long-term or chronic pain more confidently. Many people have chronic pain for many different reasons. For example:

- following an injury to bones, joints and other tissues that have healed
- after an operation
- in conditions like diabetes
- in nerve disorders like trigeminal neuralgia or peripheral neuropathy
- after a viral infection like shingles
- in different arthritis conditions like osteoarthritis or rheumatoid arthritis

It may have started gradually, like back pain or fibromyalgia, or suddenly with no clear cause. There are usually several reasons for chronic pain, rather than one specific reason.

Chronic pain has an impact on all areas of a person's life and on the people around them. This book aims to help you understand pain and its effects on your body and also looks at medical investigations and drug treatments. It covers ways of managing your activity levels, solving everyday problems, overcoming mood changes and unhelpful thinking patterns, coping with poor sleep and using relaxation techniques.

Who might benefit from using this book?

People who:

- are learning to cope with a chronic pain problem and want to be more confident about managing their lives better.
- would like to be as fit and active as possible even though they have pain.
- would like help while investigations and treatments for pain are waiting to be done or have been done.
- have found out that no more new medical treatments are likely to help.
- have a stable dose of medicines they use (if any).
- would be willing to use self-help written materials either by themselves or with support.

What does chronic pain mean?

Chronic pain problems are very common. About 10 per cent of adults in the UK are affected by pain in different parts of the body at any one time. If you have chronic pain, you will have found out that it is more than a very distressing sensation in the body. The pain can affect all aspects of you as a person and your life situation, including your feelings, your thinking, your activities, your working life, your home life, your relationships and your hobbies.

Pain is usually defined as 'an unpleasant sensory and emotional experience which is due to actual or potential tissue damage or which is expressed in terms of such damage'. Chronic pain usually means pain that has lasted for at least three months. Sometimes different words are used by healthcare professionals, such as 'long-term', 'persistent' or 'long-lasting' pain. Sometimes pain lasting six months or more is defined as chronic pain. It can be confusing, as these terms are all used to mean the same thing. The definition used in this book is pain that has lasted three months or more. Sometimes in chronic pain the nerves carrying the pain messages may have developed a 'memory' for pain that is difficult to change. This is a bit like an annoying tune that you find yourself humming all day. Sometimes the reasons for the pain are not discovered even when many tests or scans are done.

For some people, chronic pain means slight restrictions on lifestyle. For others, there may be a severe loss of independence and confidence. Pain can become long-term in spite of efforts to relieve the pain itself, or its causes if known.

People with pain problems often worry about what it means for them, their lifestyle and their future. Being limited by the effects of pain can be difficult and frustrating, especially if no 'cure' is possible. This can in turn lead to anxiety or worry and depression for some people.

What is Cognitive Behavioral Therapy?

Cognitive Behavioral Therapy (often called CBT) is a talking therapy. Talking with a trained CBT therapist helps to identify and understand what the problems are at present. This approach enables you to understand the links between body symptoms, thoughts, feelings and behavior, and how this affects your everyday life.

'Cognitive' means 'to do with thinking and beliefs'; 'behavioral' is about what we do or do not do, our behaviors or actions.

CBT was developed by Professor Aaron Beck in the 1970s, based on previous research which showed that changing the

environment and using rewards could help people to function more successfully. This was the basis for behavioral
therapies. Professor Beck demonstrated that CBT could be a
successful treatment for a number of problems, including
anxiety and depression. CBT is also useful for managing
widespread chronic pain, chronic fatigue syndrome, sleeping
problems, worry and panic attacks, anger and frustration,
severe angina and other health problems and relationship
difficulties.

Research and clinical experience with CBT has shown that
it can help people with chronic pain manage their lives better.
CBT is a practical approach to learning how to make changes
in the problems caused by the impact of chronic pain.

How can a book help?

You may have tried many different approaches to managing
your pain and you may have lots of ideas about how to deal
with the impact it has on your life. Alternatively, you may
feel completely overwhelmed and 'stuck'. Or you may just
think that a few suggestions would help. Whatever your
situation at present, this book aims to give you the tools you
need to manage your chronic pain better. Many people are
told that there is no 'relief or cure' for the pain and they will
have to 'learn to live with it'. But this can be hard if you don't
have the information and skills you need.

The chapters in this book suggest ways of overcoming low
mood, and a sense of loss and frustration. They help increase
skills to lessen worry and anxiety, deal with unhelpful
thoughts and beliefs about chronic pain. They offer ways to
talk and share issues with those close to you.

Practical problem-solving can help to increase your quality
of life. For example, you can find ways of getting necessary
things done, and doing enjoyable activities. You can set goals

and plan ways of achieving them step by step. You can also learn pacing skills to balance activity and rest. These skills will help you to gradually boost what you do, enabling you to increase your fitness without overdoing it and causing a setback.

New skills can be learned to reduce the impact of the pain. This is how a book like this can be helpful. Your pleasure and self-confidence can increase and your frustration and worry can be reduced.

A Cognitive Behavioral Therapist, a General Practitioner and a Physiotherapist have written this book jointly, with support and ideas from many confident people with chronic pain. In chronic pain services, different health professionals often work together as a team to enable people to become skilled at managing pain.

How can I get the most out of using this book?

Your pain is very personal to you. Only you know how it feels and how it affects your life. So you can use this book in the way that seems most helpful to you and your personal situation. For instance:

- The book contains a lot of questions to help you think through and apply the ideas to your own situation. If you keep a notebook close at hand, to jot down your answers, you will have a written record of your progress.
- You can read through the whole book quickly and pick up some useful tips, or you can work through more slowly – at whatever pace is best for you. When you have setbacks or flare-ups it may be helpful to work through some chapters again, learning more new tips or techniques to put into practice.

- You will probably get the most out of the book by working through a maximum of one chapter per week. Set time aside every day to work on your pain management – 20 to 30 minutes would be about right. Finding time and energy to do this can be a challenge. But it is time well spent on managing your pain better in the long term.
- You might want to work on some chapters with a friend, partner or healthcare professional. Having someone to encourage you and support you can really help but is not essential.
- Use the books, tapes, websites and organizations listed under Useful Information at the end of the book to find further specific information for your needs.

What do the chapters cover?

Part One of this book is called 'What is Chronic Pain?' and includes Chapters 1 to 5. These chapters will help you understand the impact of pain, and explain how chronic pain differs from acute pain. They also look at the roles of healthcare professionals, investigations, medicines and treatments in managing pain.

Part Two, called 'Overcoming Chronic Pain', includes Chapters 6 to 17. These practical, self-help chapters give you new approaches to think about, as well as opportunities to practise new ways of living with pain. They will help you 'learn to live with it' with more confidence.

CHAPTER 1: UNDERSTANDING THE IMPACT OF PAIN AND MAKING CHANGES

This chapter is an important introduction to the rest of the book. Understanding in more detail how chronic pain impacts on all areas of your life will help you to make the best use of the other chapters and apply them to your own situation.

CHAPTER 2: UNDERSTANDING CHRONIC PAIN AND PAIN SYSTEMS

This chapter explains what we currently understand about pain and how pain systems in the body work. Many people with chronic pain find that they can use this information to become their own 'experts' in handling their pain and its impact better.

CHAPTER 3: UNDERSTANDING INVESTIGATIONS FOR PAIN

It is likely that you will have had investigations for your pain. These might have included blood tests or x-rays or more complicated tests. This chapter explains the most common investigations and how they help healthcare professionals and the person with long-term pain.

CHAPTER 4: UNDERSTANDING THE ROLES OF HEALTHCARE PROFESSIONALS

This chapter explains the roles of healthcare professionals for people with chronic pain. This will help you access the services you need from the services available to you locally.

CHAPTER 5: UNDERSTANDING MEDICINES AND USING THEM BETTER

This chapter helps you to understand which medicines are useful for pain. It looks at how to make the best use of medicines. It also offers suggestions if you choose to stop or reduce them safely.

CHAPTER 6: SETTING GOALS

This chapter helps you set and achieve goals in different areas of your life.

CHAPTER 7: GIVING YOURSELF REWARDS

This chapter helps you understand how to use rewards for progress and efforts.

CHAPTER 8: UNDERSTANDING PACING SKILLS

This chapter explains how to plan and pace your activities every day. These are key skills to learn.

CHAPTER 9: GETTING FITTER AND BEING MORE ACTIVE

This chapter explains the importance of getting more active and how to become gradually fitter. This helps improve stamina and strength along with flexibility, so that pain limits your activities less.

CHAPTER 10: UNDERSTANDING PROBLEM-SOLVING

This chapter offers practical ways to look at and solve day-to-day difficulties.

CHAPTER 11: UNDERSTANDING SLEEP AND SLEEP PROBLEMS

This chapter looks at the kinds of sleeping difficulties people can face. It offers practical advice and ideas to help improve sleep patterns in spite of pain.

CHAPTER 12: RELAXATION

Relaxation is an important skill for people who have pain. This chapter covers how relaxation can help, and how to learn to relax.

CHAPTER 13: PAIN, COMMUNICATION AND RELATIONSHIPS

This chapter looks at the ways in which pain can affect relationships. It gives suggestions for dealing with these difficulties, including sexual problems due to pain.

CHAPTER 14: MANAGING DEPRESSION, ANXIETY AND ANGER

This chapter offers ways to try to lessen depression, anxiety and anger, as well as ways of understanding and dealing with unhelpful thinking patterns.

CHAPTER 15: ACCEPTANCE

Many people with long-term pain find that there are challenges in coming to terms with what has happened. This chapter offers some ideas that can be used in adjusting to changes in health and life circumstances.

CHAPTER 16: MAINTAINING PROGRESS AND MANAGING SETBACKS

This chapter helps build further confidence in the skills you have already learnt, to cope with pain better and deal with setbacks.

CHAPTER 17: LOOKING TO THE FUTURE AND MANAGING WORK

This chapter looks at beginning new roles or new ways of life, for example returning to work, starting a new job or retraining. It also shows you how to gather evidence of your success at managing life, despite the pain, to build up your confidence.

USEFUL INFORMATION

This section offers a range of sources of further help: books, tapes, websites, self-help groups and professional organizations.

How do I start using this book?

Following this Introduction, there is a Guide to Overcoming Chronic Pain, which explains the role of all the chapters in the book. After the Guide, there are four Case Histories, showing how pain has affected four people's lives in different ways. The people in these case histories are mentioned in many of the chapters – for example, Razia learning pacing skills in Chapter 8 and Jim trying to deal with his worries in Chapter 14 on anxiety.

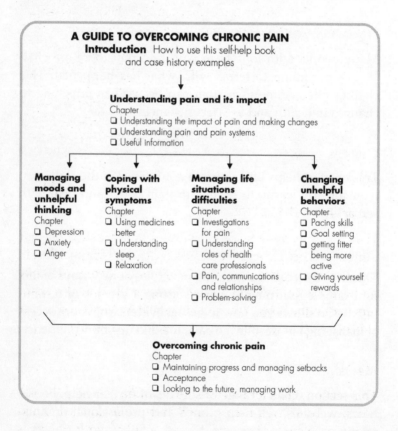

A GUIDE TO OVERCOMING CHRONIC PAIN
Introduction How to use this self-help book and case history examples

Understanding pain and its impact
Chapter
❑ Understanding the impact of pain and making changes
❑ Understanding pain and pain systems
❑ Useful information

Managing moods and unhelpful thinking
Chapter
❑ Depression
❑ Anxiety
❑ Anger

Coping with physical symptoms
Chapter
❑ Using medicines better
❑ Understanding sleep
❑ Relaxation

Managing life situations difficulties
Chapter
❑ Investigations for pain
❑ Understanding roles of health care professionals
❑ Pain, communications and relationships
❑ Problem-solving

Changing unhelpful behaviors
Chapter
❑ Pacing skills
❑ Goal setting
❑ getting fitter being more active
❑ Giving yourself rewards

Overcoming chronic pain
Chapter
❑ Maintaining progress and managing setbacks
❑ Acceptance
❑ Looking to the future, managing work

- You may find it helpful to start by reading the first two chapters, which are aimed at everyone with chronic pain. Chapter 1 will give an opportunity to set your own targets for change. Then Chapter 2 will give you the background knowledge you need, explaining more about acute and chronic pain.
- After that, you can choose the most relevant chapters for your own needs or targets for change, using the Guide to Overcoming Chronic Pain (see p. 10) to guide you. You can use this guide to help you work through the book, ticking off the chapters as you read them.
- Alternatively, you could start by reading the case histories and trying to find an example that seems to relate to your difficulties and needs. Later you can track how these individuals make changes in the different chapters and experiment with the new skills they learn.

Four case histories

Here are some case history examples to show how chronic pain affects people and their lives in different ways. You can follow these people and their progress in learning to cope and become confident with their pain in the different chapters within the book. You will also see how they try out new skills to help reduce the impact of pain on their lives.

Maria

I am useless, I cannot do anything anymore
Maria, aged 47, was a school meals service cook. She has had a pain problem for three years since a fall at work. She lives

alone now. She used to be married but was physically abused by her ex-husband and divorced him 20 years ago while her children were young. All her four children live nearby. She has seen several hospital specialists and her GP. She has been told that she has a bulging disc, osteoporosis and spondylosis. She does not really know what is wrong or what these labels or diseases mean. She is frightened that her spine may wear out. She is concerned that she will have more pain and end up bed-ridden like her mother.

Pain sites: Maria has had pain in her neck, left shoulder and arm since her fall.

Pacing of activities: On bad pain days, Maria often spends most of the day in a chair or in bed. On better days, she tries to get everything done that she has had to put off for so long. She finds the next day she is very tired and the pain can be severe.

Mood changes: Maria realizes she has changed. She used to be a bright, cheerful, amiable person, who loved her job and would help others out. Now she often cannot be bothered to tidy the house, cook meals for herself, or look after the garden. She can be very tearful, moans out loud a lot and gets very angry, even violent at times with herself or with other people.

She blames herself for rushing at work, so causing the fall in the first place.

Relationships: The family are at a loss, as Maria is often grumpy. She often shouts at them when things are left lying around the house after their visits. Maria realizes how it affects them and is frightened that they will stop visiting her. She says, 'It is the pain, it has so changed my life, I hate it.' She misses her work colleagues. She would love to get back to work but does not know how, or what she can do to help herself.

Razia

I can't get to do things; the pain spoils every day

Razia is 28 years old, with two young sons aged five and seven. She is married to Hassian, who is a postal worker. He leaves for work early in the morning, sometimes six days a week. This means leaving Razia to get the children up and take them to the nearby school. Razia's elderly parents live next-door. They both have difficulty walking because of arthritis in their knees and back.

Pain sites: Razia has chronic widespread pain mainly in the neck, both shoulders and lower back. The pain moves around her body and some days she has severe headaches. Razia finds that each day is different, as she does not know where the pain will be the next day. 'I can't plan anything,' she says.

Physical function: In the morning, Razia's stiffness can be very severe. Razia finds that some of her daily routines make this stiffness much worse, e.g. bathing her youngest child. Razia has difficulty managing her pain, especially when her pain levels are high. This means that her physical functioning is limited. She says, 'I rest until the pain settles which could be a couple of days. This means I get so little done in the house.'

Pacing of activities: Razia finds her pain and stiffness very unpredictable and says that it is hard for her to plan and pace her days. Razia tends to rest as much as possible to save her energy and lessen her pain levels. She does this so that when her husband and children come home she can 'see to them'.

Sleep problems: Razia complains that she has difficulty dropping off to sleep because she can't get comfortable. She sleeps about six hours a night but wakes up feeling tired most mornings: 'I'm as tired as when I went to bed last night.' Razia says she feels 'tired all of the time'. She often has a couple of short sleep breaks during the day but still finds she has little energy and is very irritable with the children, which upsets her a lot.

Medication: Razia has been given Amitriptyline, 10 mg daily. This helps her sleep better but she doesn't like the drowsy feeling the next day. She only takes the medication if her husband is having a day off work, so that he can look after the children.

Relationships: Razia relies heavily on her husband and children to help her out. When her husband is at work, she says, 'My children have to put my shoes on for me.' Hassian, her husband, can't understand what is wrong and is beginning to ask why things aren't done when he gets home. There is a family wedding in two months' time and Razia's mother sometimes expects her to do things to help her out. This is an added stress, especially when Razia has a bad pain day. Razia finds it difficult to refuse her mother's requests.

Mood changes: Razia was very low after the birth of her second child. She is beginning to have the same depressed feelings again. She worries about the pain and what it might mean for her and her family in the future. She is frustrated that 'I can't do the same things that I used to, like cooking and swimming.'

Previous treatment: Razia was seeing a physiotherapist who gave her some stretches to loosen her muscles. She stopped going after two sessions, as the physiotherapist 'wasn't helping my pain at all'.

Jim

Why won't the pain leave me?

Jim has severe pain around the left side of his chest and abdomen after an attack of shingles (herpes zoster) five years ago. He is married to Ann, and they have had a close relationship over their thirty years of marriage. Jim is 59 and his pain problem has made him tired and worried. It made sense to both Ann and Jim for him to retire from his job as a secondary school teacher over two years ago. It had been a difficult time, with many stresses in his life over the last three years. These included his long-term pain after his shingles, his early retirement, Ann's heart condition and the death of his elderly parents. Since his retirement, Jim has taken on many household tasks to fill his day. This has also helped Ann because some days she is short of breath because of her heart problems.

Pain sites: Jim finds the stinging pain around the left side of his abdomen and his left shoulder blade area unbearable at times. His skin is extremely sensitive and irritable, and his clothes feel very uncomfortable on his skin. He is frightened of anyone coming close to him on the left side in case they touch him. He sometimes moves out of the way when people come towards him on his left-hand side.

Pacing: Jim tries to do everything himself. He shops every day for food and he cooks most of the meals. He does all the vacuuming, washing and ironing and most of the other housework. Ann and Jim have a large garden. Jim usually spends the rest of his time weeding, planting out and mowing the lawn. He thinks that this is only fair as he is not working any more and Ann is sometimes quite unwell. He likes to feel useful and that he has achieved something every day. He says, 'It helps to keep busy, as it takes my mind off the pain.'

Sleep problems: Jim is tired when he goes to bed. He has difficulty getting off to sleep as he thinks over recent events and worries about what the future holds. He would like to sleep in. However Ann often gets up very early, around 6 a.m. and Jim thinks he should start his day at that time too. He is quite groggy in the morning but he tries to be bright and cheerful for Ann. He is not sure how she would cope if he seemed depressed. Jim notices that when he is tired, his pain seems worse.

Medication: Jim no longer wants to take his medication because 'it doesn't work and he wants to feel in control'. He is worried that if he does take tablets he will 'become addicted'. He saw his mother become dependent on tranquillizers and he's 'not going to become like her'.

Relationships: Jim feels irritable and stressed because of the high standards that he sets himself. He is worried about the future, especially at times when the pain is severe. He doesn't know if he can continue at this pace for much longer. He doesn't want to let Ann know his worries: 'She has enough problems without worrying about me.' His skin is so sensitive that he is often frightened of being hugged by his grandchildren or by Ann. This upsets Ann as it makes her feel less close to Jim, just when she feels worried because of her illness.

Mood changes: Jim is aware that he is having difficulty relaxing and it has been getting worse recently. He used to enjoy walking and reading. But he can't seem to find the time now, especially as Ann's health recently had a setback. He is worried that if the pain gets worse he won't be able to manage: 'What will happen to us then?'

Previous treatment: Jim has been to the pain clinic and had medication and acupuncture. He is not sure why the treatments haven't worked and why the nerve pain does not settle down.

Steve

Why can't they fix the pain?
Steve is 26 and used to be a very active cyclist and runner and loved canoeing. He was an electronic technician and was

due for promotion. He used to cycle to work most days. One day a car hit him from behind while he was waiting at a pedestrian crossing. He was thrown from his bike and landed awkwardly on his back. He felt something in his back split. He was stunned but was able to get up and walk about. His bike was smashed beyond repair. He went for a hospital check-up and there was no evidence of any fractures or serious damage. He was advised to rest and was given some pain relief drugs. For several days he had pain in his back, then it seemed to improve. After two weeks he decided he would go back to work but the pain started to get much worse. His back and leg movements were much stiffer and at the end of the working day he had to go to bed. After two months he could not manage work anymore. He has not been able to cycle since the accident. He can only hobble around the house. He has started to get up much later each morning, and finds that lying down helps ease his pain.

Pain sites: About 18 months after the accident, Steve's pain was in his lower back and had spread into his left leg and his right shoulder. He sometimes had pins and needles in his right arm and his left knee would give way.

Mood changes: Steve is getting very frustrated. He has lost his job and is not able to do his hobbies. He often thinks about all the things he used to do, like mountain biking on Saturdays. He isn't able to join in the local bike race events anymore. He wanted to go back to karate classes and has not been able to get there. He often thinks, 'It's not fair that I have this pain. It was that driver's fault. He blamed me for stopping for the pedestrian crossing.' Steve has been fed-up about the long wait to see the specialist. He eventually had an MRI scan of his back, but the scan showed no evidence of spinal problems in his discs or bones. This made him even angrier. He would shout at Nicole, his girlfriend. He sometimes drinks too much beer as it helps his pain and calms him down. He then seems to get snappier the next day. 'I just want to do the things I used to do, I am not going to go on living like this.'

Relationships: Steve's mood changes have been affecting Nicole, who has been getting really worried about him. Steve seems to be less physically close to Nicole. He often sleeps in the spare bedroom. This means he can get up in the night and use the computer. This has helped him, as he has found some useful websites for pain sufferers. He can use their chat rooms to find out more about pain. This upsets Nicole, as she seems to be living in the day and Steve seems to be living in the night. If Nicole tries to talk about it with Steve he just says it is the pain and he can't cope any other way.

Previous treatment: Steve has tried at least six or seven different drugs for his pain but he finds that they only work for the first two or three weeks. Then their pain relief effect lessens. His GP can only suggest more tablets and Steve is not keen to try anymore. He is fed up with the side-effects, especially constipation and a dry mouth. He hates eating fruit to help his constipation. He enjoys his takeaways, especially fish and chips, as this seems to be his only pleasure. But he does not like the fact that he has put on about 30 lb.

Sleep problems: Nicole has noticed that Steve is a very restless sleeper and often has bad dreams or nightmares, sometimes breaking out into sweats. This means that he will sleep in until midday and sometimes stay in his bedroom, near the toilet, until late afternoon.

Physical function: Some days, Steve finds it almost impossible to climb the stairs. He tells Nicole, 'I am not coming downstairs. I'm staying in the bedroom – it is close to the toilet.' He finds a walking stick helpful but refuses to go to the shops on bad days if he has to use it: 'Other people think I have a glass back.'

Legal and financial issues: Steve has decided to sue the driver because of all the problems he has had since the accident. He has now seen six different specialists for his legal case. He is very confused about why he still has the pain. His solicitor wants him to see a psychologist about his nightmares and angry moods. Nicole and Steve are also beginning to struggle financially. Their credit card and electric bills are overdue. Nicole only works part-time. Steve is worried about how they are going to pay their bills. They have already had a loan from Steve's mother and just don't know what to do next.

PART ONE

What is Chronic Pain?

1

Understanding the impact of pain and making changes

This chapter aims to help you understand:

- How pain has taken over parts of your life.
- How to change the impact of chronic pain.
- How it is possible to live life fully despite pain.
- The advantages and disadvantages of making changes.

How far has pain taken control of you and your life?

Your pain is real and is probably having a big impact on you right now – on your activities, your moods, your thinking and how you see the future.

Put a mark X on the line below to indicate how far pain is controlling you:

1	2	3	4	5	6	7	8	9	10
Not at all									Totally

Asking some questions will help you identify the problems or difficulties that your pain has caused you. Getting to know what your problems are is the first step towards learning to manage your pain. Once you know what the problems are, then you can see what to change.

This book will help you to be more confident in knowing how to manage the problems and make simple changes happen yourself. In other words, you can begin to take back control of your life. The changes may not be easy to make at first, but they will be worth it in the end.

People who have been on pain management courses have found that understanding **what** are the problems and learning **how** to manage them has meant better days, better nights and generally better times in their lives. They have become more confident in managing their lives despite the pain.

> *I can now cope with family life much better. I know more about dealing with the pain, I am more in control of it. My confidence has really grown in my new skills, like pacing my day and night, using relaxation and dealing with worries. I see myself being better at coping, better to live with, my husband has a new wife again. I can live life to the full again but very differently.*
>
> *Previous pain sufferer*

Using the person-centred model

Using the model or guide shown on the next page can be helpful. It describes the five parts of a whole person and is known as a person-centred model. The model will help you and others to understand you as a person and the impact the pain has on you **now**.

PERSON-CENTRED MODEL

Body symptoms
(Type of pain or sensation)

Moods
(Emotions)

Thoughts
(Thinking in words or pictures, memories and beliefs or rules)

Behaviors
(What you do or do not do)

Present/past life situation
(Environment, work, relationships, etc)

An example of the impact of chronic pain on a person using the model:

Maria and the person-centred model

You may find it helpful to consider Maria's case history in relation to the person-centred model, in order to understand the impact of chronic pain on Maria and her life.

Maria, aged 47, used to be a school meals service cook. She has had a pain problem for three years since a fall at work. She lives alone now. She used to be married but was physically abused by her ex-husband and divorced him 20 years ago while her children were young. All her four children live nearby. She has seen several hospital specialists and her GP. She has been told that she has a bulging disc, osteoporosis and spondylosis. She does not really know what is wrong or what these labels or diseases mean.

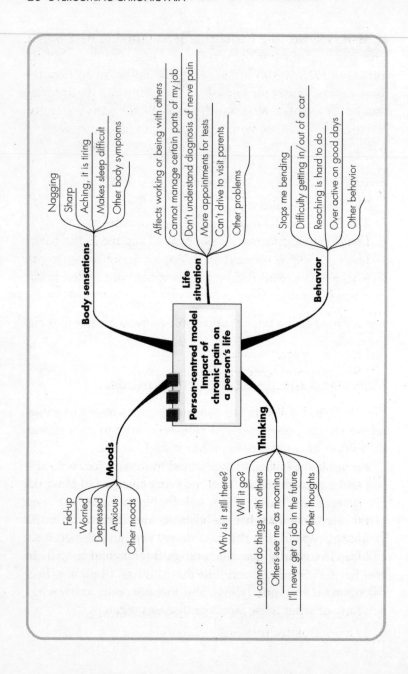

Body sensations
- Nagging
- Sharp
- Aching, it is tiring
- Makes sleep difficult
- Other body symptoms

Life situation
- Affects working or being with others
- Cannot manage certain parts of my job
- Don't understand diagnosis of nerve pain
- More appointments for tests
- Can't drive to visit parents
- Other problems

Behavior
- Stops me bending
- Difficulty getting in/out of a car
- Reaching is hard to do
- Over active on good days
- Other behavior

Person-centred model
Impact of
chronic pain on
a person's life

Moods
- Fed-up
- Worried
- Depressed
- Anxious
- Other moods

Thinking
- Why is it still there?
- Will it go?
- I cannot do things with others
- Others see me as moaning
- I'll never get a job in the future
- Other thoughts

Maria realizes she has changed. She used to be a bright, cheerful, amiable person, who loved her job and would help others out. Now she often cannot be bothered to tidy the house, cook meals for herself, or look after the garden. She can be very tearful, moans out loud a lot and gets very angry, even violent at times with herself or with other people.

She completed the person-centred model like this:

BODY SYMPTOMS

The pain 'crucifies me'.
The tablets 'make me a zombie' and constipated.
I have severe spasms 'like a horse kicked me in the back'.
I have sleep problems, waking up to five times each night.
My back is so stiff I sometimes can't get out of bed in the morning.

MOODS

I feel angry and frustrated.
I feel depressed and hopeless at times.
I feel so frightened, especially about the future.
I am embarrassed.

THOUGHTS

I don't want to be a wimp; I used to be a strong person.
I would top myself if I went into a home, it would end the pain.
I try not to take tablets, as it means I can't stand the pain.
I hate people doing things for me. I do things for others.
Others see me as moaning and getting violent.

BEHAVIORS (WHAT YOU DO OR DON'T DO)

I spend 70 per cent of the day in a chair or in bed.
I rarely cook for myself these days.

I am in tears a lot.

I am always grumpy and shouting, especially with the family.

I have lost my job and my work friends. I have far less money. I have always worked seven days a week, and I don't now.

I am stuck at home; I can't get out alone, so it's the same four walls every day.

I used to love going dancing, sometimes five times a week.

My neighbours now check on me in case I have fallen or I am stuck on the toilet.

My family don't understand what is happening to me.

I survived as a single parent, but this pain beats me.

The specialist never saw me after the scan test.

The model shows how the pain has taken over Maria's life. This person-centred model also helps to show what can be changed. A helpful change in any of the five parts or categories can lead to changes in the other parts.

The person-centred model can also help to highlight other difficulties that are not obviously linked to the pain.

How did the model help Maria make changes for the better?

Problem: Maria had stiffness in her back (**body symptom**), especially in the mornings, so she had great difficulty getting out of bed.

Change: She made a change in her **behavior**. She started trying to do a few specific stretch and strength exercises to ease her back stiffness while in bed in the morning.

Result: This helped reduce the stiffness and getting out of bed was 50 per cent easier for Maria. She felt less frightened (**mood**) and more confident (**mood**). She started to think that she could manage and not rely as much on help from others (**thought**).

Problem: Maria felt depressed (**mood**) because she thought she could not manage at home (**thought**).

Change: She changed her **behavior**. She started to keep a record of the times she did manage her days fairly well.

Result: The evidence from this record helped her to feel less depressed (**mood**) despite her pain. It was evidence that she did manage many days fairly well.

Maria's list of problems due to pain became her **targets for change**:

- Pain in my back
- My stiff back and neck in the mornings
- Difficulty getting out of bed/climbing the stairs/ hanging out the washing
- Sleep problems – waking with pain/not being able to turn over
- Mood changes – feeling depressed/feeling angry/ feeling frightened and thinking I will fall and get stuck on the toilet
- No social life – no dancing/spending all day on my own
- Can't understand why the pains won't go away
- Scan result – what did it say? What does the result mean?

How can the person-centred model help you get ready tomake some changes?

You can use the blank person-centred model below as a guide to work out what difficulties pain causes you and how your pain affects your life. Filling in each section will give you a list of problems to think about, so that you can decide what you really want to change. It may help to look back at how Maria filled in the person-centred model earlier.

PERSON-CENTRED MODEL
Body symptoms (Type of pain or body sensation)
Moods (Emotions)
Thoughts (Words, pictures, memories, beliefs or rules)
Behaviors (What you do or don't do)
Your present/past life situation (Environment, work, relationships, etc)

Now you can look at your problem list and decide what changes you want to make.

A problem list can help you (and your family and friends) see which of your problems are mainly due to pain.

Ask yourself: What are the main difficulties at present which I would value changing or improving?

Tick the difficulties you want to change or improve:

- ❑ Problems with walking and moving about
- ❑ Problems with balance
- ❑ Lack of fitness and energy
- ❑ Side-effects or problems with current medicines for pain
- ❑ Unhelpful pacing (a pattern of doing too much, getting more pain, then doing too little and resting)
- ❑ Insufficient pain relief
- ❑ Not understanding why long-term pain occurs
- ❑ Disturbed sleep
- ❑ Moods, e.g. depression, guilt, anger or anxiety/worry
- ❑ Relationship difficulties because of pain
- ❑ Sexual problems
- ❑ Not being able to work or continue working
- ❑ Financial difficulties
- ❑ Resolving legal claims
- ❑ Other difficulties that are important to change (write them down in your notebook)

Do you know what you would want to change from this list? If not, it may help to share your list with someone else. Maria saw her GP, who helped her work through her problem list. Other people you could work with include physiotherapists, practice or specialist nurses, occupational therapists, community mental health nurses, pharmacists, family members, friends, work colleagues, local pain support group members and local health fitness centres.

If you ticked more than three areas of your life above think about which three areas you would value changing most. Choose, even if only little changes are possible now.

Write these changes in your notebook:

These are your **targets for change** and will help you draw up an action plan.

Avoid the wish list trap. People often say to themselves: 'All of it!!!' Well, that is not possible or realistic. But it *is* possible to make little changes even in the biggest problems – just as it is possible to build a big house, one brick at a time.

Getting started

When you have been in pain for a long time, it is sometimes difficult to know where to start and what to do to change the situation. People can often be held back by fears about becoming more disabled or being a burden, doing themselves harm or the pain getting worse. These concerns can lead them to overdo activities, battle on and then have a setback. They can also lead them to avoid doing things and limit activities more than is needed.

Managing pain includes taking into account what is happening *now*. Sometimes it is very difficult to face up to the idea that you cannot do everything the way you used to (see Chapter 8 on Pacing).

Reducing the impact of pain on your daily life

Using your three **targets to change**, write down in your notebook what you would most like to change about your 'typical day'.

What three things would be different if you managed your pain and life better?

Write down in your notebook what you would most like to change to achieve your targets:

- What physical activities would you change?
- What about enjoyable things (like hobbies)?

In reaching these targets, who would you spend more or less time with?

More time with	Less time with
e.g. my daughter	e.g. the doctor

After you have written down your ideas, write down what would be **better** if things were different:

- What would be better about social activities?
- What would be better about household tasks?
- What else?

How do you or others see these changes occurring?

When you have put down your ideas, it is helpful to see that there are some points in favour of doing things in a different way.

Next, see if you can think of any advantages of things staying the way they are now. This may seem like a strange idea, but you may have concerns or worries about changing. These also need to be thought about.

What could be positive about not changing things?

For instance:

- It can simply seem too hard to make changes.
- It is nice to have people who look after us when we are ill.
- It can be an advantage not to have to go out with family.

Next, write in your notebook four reasons for things staying the same. Small or silly reasons are fine, as well as important ones.

Have a look at what you have written down so far, and think about the advantages and disadvantages of putting effort into changing. When everyday things are already difficult, it is important to have good reasons to try something new.

Now think about your **most important** reasons for changing, and your **main concerns** about what this would involve.

Write them in your notebook:

Do you have other concerns? If so, make a note of them in your notebook:

Now, spend a little time thinking about what you can and **do** manage. Try not to compare yourself with how you used to be before your pain. This can be quite a challenge! What are your strengths? Try to write down at least three. (The more you can find, the better you are likely to feel.)

What helps you to keep going? Write down at least three things.

Now you have had time to think about the advantages and possible disadvantages of making changes, think about how important it is to you that things change.

Put a mark X on the line below to indicate how **important** it is to you that your three identified targets from page 31 change.

1	2	3	4	5	6	7	8	9	10

Not at
all important

Extremely
important

Put a mark X on the line below to indicate how confident you are about changing your targets.

1	2	3	4	5	6	7	8	9	10

Not at
all confident

Extremely
confident

Put a mark X on the line below to indicate how **ready** you are to change **now**.

1	2	3	4	5	6	7	8	9	10

Not at
all ready

Extremely
ready to change

CHAPTER SUMMARY

- Pain can affect all five parts of a person: their body symptoms, their moods, their thoughts, their behaviors and their life situation.
- Understanding the impact of chronic pain will help you to be clear about your targets to change.
- It is important to focus on what can be changed, as the pain itself is often not very easy to change.
- In order to get started, you need to be clear about the advantages and disadvantages of making changes for yourself.

- Working through different chapters in this book will help you find out how to make these changes. You can choose to do this either alone or with support from a partner, family, friends or a healthcare professional.

2

Understanding chronic pain and pain systems

This chapter aims to help you understand more about:

- The two types of pain, acute and chronic
- Pain systems in the body
- The different theories of pain, including the Gate Control Theory of Pain

Understanding pain

Chronic pain problems are very common. As many as 1 in 7 people are affected by chronic pain, often in different parts of their bodies. Pain is a very personal experience and only you really know how your own pain feels. It can be difficult to find words to describe it to other people. This can make it hard for them to understand how distressing your pain is for you.

Think about how you would describe your pain to someone. For instance, you might use words that describe the **pain sensation**, such as 'sharp', 'shooting', 'nagging' or 'aching'. Or you might use words to describe how it **makes you feel**, such as 'worried', 'scared', 'angry', 'down', 'guilty' or 'fed up'. You might also include phrases describing what you **think** about your pain such as:

- *I knew I shouldn't have lifted that heavy container at work.*
- *Pain means I've been injured. It hurts, so I shouldn't move.*
- *Headaches run in my family. I knew I would get them some time.*
- *Bad backs never get better.*
- *It's a damaged nerve after the shingles. It must be serious!*

You might also say that you have to **do things differently or stop doing** activities

- *I am unable to bend and pick things up from the floor.*
- *It alters the way I move – I walk much more stiffly.*
- *The pain makes me lie down more often.*
- *It stops me going out with friends.*

1 Look at the pain diagram opposite and circle the words that describe your pain.
2 Add any other words that you use to describe your pain.
3 Add a new branch to the diagram if you need to.

Pain affects you as a person in many ways.

Look at the impact of pain diagram on page 41. Add anything to it that you think has been missed out.

Acute and chronic pain

A worldwide group of pain specialists (International Association for Study of Pain (IASP) define pain as:

An unpleasant sensory and emotional experience which is due to actual or potential tissue damage or which is expressed in terms of such damage.

This is the definition most doctors and other health professionals use when assessing pain problems.

Doctors, nurses and physiotherapists used to think that pain systems in the body were very simple. However, we now understand that the experience of pain is much more complex. Current research in pain is focusing on how the body's pain systems work. This will help doctors find ways to reduce pain levels in the future.

What is acute pain?

If you twist an ankle or slip and fall on your knees you will feel acute pain as the muscles, tendons, ligaments, bones, nerves or skin are damaged. You may see a bruise or swelling, and you may feel a lot of pain at the site where the injury has happened. The body releases chemicals and diverts blood to the area in order to help repair damaged tissue. Most pain symptoms usually reduce over six weeks as tissues heal. Nearly all injured tissues are fully healed at six months.

What is chronic pain?

This is pain that continues for longer than three months and it is not normally associated with damaged tissues. We know that all the body's tissues, even broken bones, are usually healed after six months.

Healthcare professionals believe that this type of pain persists for longer than the usual three-month healing period. This is because the nerves originally carrying the pain

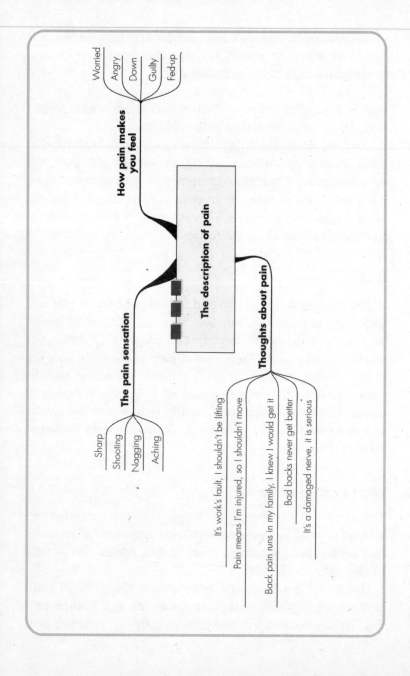

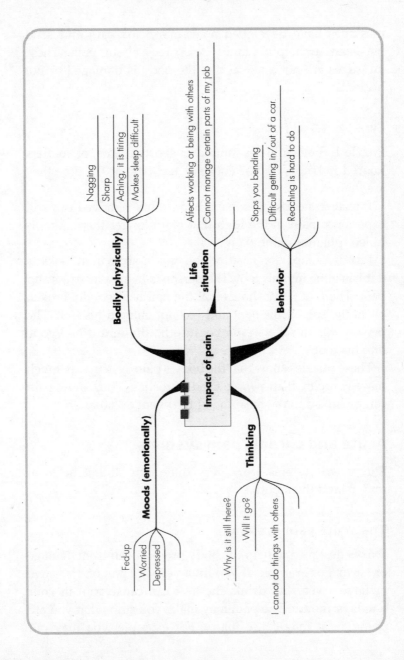

messages have developed a 'memory' for pain and send persistent unhelpful 'faulty' messages about pain. These messages are not a signal that the body is damaged or not healed.

Puzzle 1: Some athletes injured in sports events, or soldiers injured in battle, do not notice or feel pain at the time they are injured.

Puzzle 2: People who have had a limb removed can still experience pain in the limb that is no longer there. This is called 'phantom limb pain'.

Puzzle 3: A person has trodden on a sharp nail. It looks as if it has gone into his foot. The person is in great distress and pain. The foot x-ray shows that the nail has actually broken off in the sole of his boot and has not entered his foot. The person was in severe pain because he **thought** it had gone into his foot.

These puzzles show that the body's pain systems are much more complex than people used to realize. They show pain can be linked to the meaning of the event or situation.

Acute and chronic pain systems

These two systems work very differently and it helps to understand them both.

The acute pain system

This is designed to help the body protect itself from damage or harm. For example, if you lift a very hot pan off the stove or have a very hot drink, the heat can cause pain in your hands or mouth. The pain may make you stop what you are doing, as it may cause injury. For example, you may put down the pan, or sometimes even drop it, to avoid being injured by the painful heat.

Acute pain nerve fibres take the pain message from the injury as fast as possible through the spinal cord to the pain centres in the brain. This is a survival mechanism designed to protect the body so the nerves need to send messages quickly to that part of the body to do something immediately, e.g. remove the hand from the hot pan. These are called 'A' nerve fibres (standing for 'acute fast pain message system'). You can think of this system as being similar to dialling straight through to the emergency services for immediate action.

The chronic pain system

This system works differently from the acute pain system. It sends messages to the pain centres in the brain via another type of pain nerve fibre – 'C' fibres (standing for 'chronic pain system'). These fibres send messages very slowly and repeatedly to several pain centres in the brain.

The brain may interpret these persistent pain messages to mean that the pain problem is still happening and is not finished or healed. Alternatively, the 'C' fibres may develop a 'memory' for pain experiences, and continue to send pain messages for many months or years after an injury, when healing is complete. These fibres are like a set of traffic lights stuck on red, which cannot switch onto green.

The 'C' fibre nerve endings can become very sensitive to movement, hot and cold sensations and chemical changes (like inflammation within the body system). Sometimes if the pain area is touched or moved, they send off many, many pain messages to the brain. The nerves seem to magnify the pain feelings or intensity, or cause other sensations like numbness or tingling.

So there seem to be many problems at different places – in the nerve endings, the nerve fibres and the pain centres in the brain. The important point is that feeling chronic pain does not mean there is any harm or damage happening in the body. These are unhelpful 'faulty' messages about pain or body sensations, which the pain centres in the brain treat as if they were accurate.

In addition, scar tissue from healed tissues can become tight and stiff. The pain nerves may be wrapped within this tissue. When moving this part of the body, the lack of flexibility (especially in muscles, tendons or joints) can increase pain messages.

There is some good news. It is possible to increase flexibility in stiff, tight tissues and thereby reduce the pain and its consequences. Gradually stretching and strengthening helps the nerve fibres become less sensitive to movement, enabling you to be more active and in less pain.

The best that doctors and physiotherapists can do is to try to help the person to control the pain, possibly by using medications and other treatments (see Chapter 5). However, this may only change the pain experience a little or in the short term. Doctors and pain scientists still don't know enough about chronic pain systems and how to switch off the 'C' fibre pain messages. This means it is difficult to change:

- the memory of pain in the 'C' fibres and the pain centres in the brain
- the increased sensitivity in these nerve endings
- With acute pain or during a setback, it is sensible to reduce many activities for two or three days, especially if there is a lot of bruising or swelling.
- Most active sports people reduce their sports activities and have longer rest periods. Then, after two or three

days, they gradually start to do more, steadily pacing and planning their increased activities (see Chapter 8).

- Rest, especially complete rest in bed, is now believed to cause more problems than it solves, except in certain situations, such as cases of severe multiple injuries, e.g. after a car accident.

TABLE 2.1: SHOULD I REST AND TAKE IT EASY IF I HAVE A PAIN PROBLEM?

Activity	Acute pain	Chronic pain
Rest in bed	No	No
Potter at own pace	Yes	Yes
Increase activity steadily	Yes	Yes
Cut down on all activities	No	No
Cut down some activities if bad pain period	Yes	Yes

Theories of pain

The Gate Control Theory of Pain

In the 1960s, two scientists, called Ronald Melzack and Patrick Wall, carried out research to understand pain systems. They developed the Gate Control Theory of Pain.

According to this theory, there are 'gates' in the nerve junctions, spinal cord and pain centres in the brain. These gates open and let pain messages through the pain system, so that we feel pain. They can also close to stop messages going through the system, so that the pain is reduced or stopped.

In the 1970s, it was discovered that the body can make its own pain-relief chemicals. These are called endorphins and they work like the pain-relieving drug, morphine. The endorphins can help close the gate. This may explain why some athletes sometimes do not feel pain, even when they are stretching themselves to the limit while doing their sport. Physical activity increases endorphin levels in the body, giving a feeling of well-being and helping to close the pain gate.

In chronic pain there are no treatments that can shut the gate and keep it closed all the time. However, there are ways to close the gate as much as possible so that fewer pain messages pass through the pain system. The brain can focus on very distracting activities. So, for example, someone scoring a winning goal, can have a painful muscle injury and not be aware of much pain.

You can use the skills described in Part Two of this book to gain some control over how much the gate is open or closed. In this way, pain can become more manageable and your life more active.

Other theories of pain

Our understanding about chronic pain and theories about its development are constantly changing. One emerging theory is based on the neuromatrix. This theory helps explain the complex changes that occur in the body's nerve and sensory system for pain as these systems adapt and evolve to deal successfully with threats. This newer theory helps us understand further why getting good pain relief is so difficult. It explains why there are many different problems in different sites, including the brain's centres for processing and interpreting pain messages. This theory likens the brain's pain centres to an orchestra, with different groups of instruments trying to play music without a conductor. It highlights the importance of developing coping skills to manage your activities, moods and unhelpful thinking so that you are in control of the pain and independent, and the pain is not in control of you.

WHAT CLOSES THE GATE AND STOPS PAIN?

Circle those things or activities that you know affect your own gate and add more if you can on page 48.

WHAT OPENS THE GATE AND LETS PAIN THROUGH?

Circle those things or activities that you know affect your own gate and add more if you can.

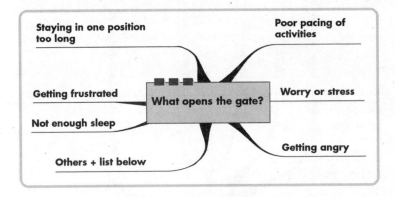

WHAT OTHER PARTS OF THE BODY CAN SEND PAIN MESSAGES?

The human body is a complex, tough structure, designed to heal itself while still being active. Our bodies are made up of tissues that help them to move: bones, joints and cartilage; muscles and tendons; ligaments; nerves and nerve receptors; and blood vessels.

- **Bones** are strong supporting structures, linked to each other by thick, strong, elastic tissues called ligaments.
- **Joints** are places where two bones meet (for example, the shoulder joint, which allows big movements in many directions). Other joints move in fewer directions (like the knee joint, which moves in just two directions).

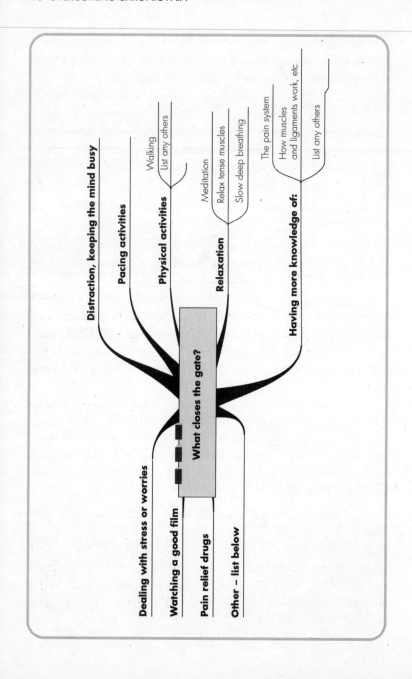

Distraction, keeping the mind busy

Pacing activities

Physical activities
- Walking
- List any others

Relaxation
- Meditation
- Relax tense muscles
- Slow deep breathing

Having more knowledge of:
- The pain system
- How muscles and ligaments work, etc
- List any others

What closes the gate?

Dealing with stress or worries

Watching a good film

Pain relief drugs

Other – list below

- **Cartilage** lines the ends of the long bones, e.g. the thigh bone, and helps with smooth movement during activity.
- **Muscles** provide power to move the body via joints and to keep it upright. Muscles are very strongly fixed to the bones and around joints by tendons. There are many large and small muscles in the body that are arranged in layers, a bit like an onion.

WHAT HAPPENS TO THESE TISSUES WHEN THEY ARE INJURED?

Following injury, muscles become tight to protect the body and prevent movement for a short time – perhaps hours or days. This helps the body's healing process.

In chronic pain, when the pain does not reduce, then muscles may stay very tense. The person may be fearful of the pain and avoid being active and stretching. Gradually, over several days and weeks, the muscles, together with the ligaments and tendons, become short and stiff and feel very tight.

The vicious circle shown overleaf may help to explain why people often say, for instance, 'the pain started in my lower arm and has now gone into other areas'.

Frequently asked questions

Q. Is it possible to loosen stiff, tight, painful muscles and joints?
A. It is possible to loosen many joints in the body, and lengthen and strengthen muscles, through gradual exercises and stretches (see Chapter 9). Learning relaxation skills helps the muscles to 'let go' again and become supple and flexible.

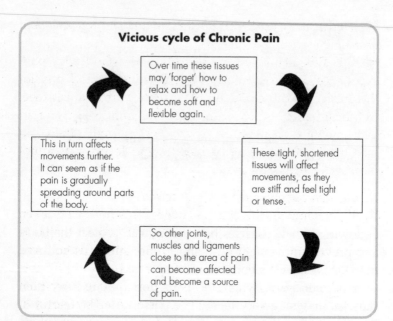

Vicious cycle of Chronic Pain

Over time these tissues may 'forget' how to relax and how to become soft and flexible again.

These tight, shortened tissues will affect movements, as they are stiff and feel tight or tense.

So other joints, muscles and ligaments close to the area of pain can become affected and become a source of pain.

This in turn affects movements further. It can seem as if the pain is gradually spreading around parts of the body.

Q. If chronic pain cannot be relieved, then what?
A. It is possible to make day-to-day life more manageable despite the pain. In Part Two of this book, you will learn skills that will enable you to:

- Feel less frustrated, worried and depressed
- Be more physically active
- Use medicines in helpful ways
- Have more of a social life with family and friends
- Become more independent in everyday activities
- Manage setbacks confidently
- Become better at planning, pacing and prioritizing activities

Q. Why is it difficult for doctors to understand my pain problem?

A. It is difficult for anyone to truly understand your pain experience. It can seem invisible. For doctors and physiotherapists, it is more difficult because they are unable to see, feel, hear, smell, touch or measure the pain itself using an instrument, a scan or an x-ray. For example, they can measure blood pressure or blood sugar levels but cannot measure or scan pain itself.

Q. Why don't people take my pain seriously?

A. It can sometimes feel as if your pain is not being taken seriously. Most health professionals will believe that it is very distressing and disabling for you. Family, friends and health professionals will often be frustrated at not being able to change things for you. You could perhaps check whether they understand about the different pain systems. If not, you can use the information in this chapter. It may help them understand more about pain systems, the difficulties caused by chronic pain, how they affect you and ways to manage pain.

You could also write down a list of questions to ask your doctor or physiotherapist about the pain and your body's pain systems.

CHAPTER SUMMARY

- Chronic pain is a different pain system in the body from acute pain. This helps to explain why pain symptoms can continue for many months or years and be difficult to relieve.
- There is no clear link between the level or amount of pain experienced and tissue damage or injury.
- The Gate Control Theory of Pain helps to explain what factors can change the pain experience. Identifying what helps close your own 'gates' on pain messages can help you manage pain better. The

euro-matrix theory begins to unravel some of the problems in the pain systems, which are complex but emphasize being in control of pain by using specific skills.

- Muscles, joints and ligaments can lose their flexibility and become stiff and tight. These factors also help to explain why pain can sometimes persist.

3

Understanding investigations for pain

This chapter aims to help you:

- Understand more about investigations for chronic pain, such as blood tests, x-rays and scans
- Ask questions and talk about these investigations with your doctor
- Make sense of test results, both positive and negative
- Find ways to cope with waiting for investigations and results

Blood tests

Blood tests can help doctors find the causes of some diseases or health problems. But, in almost all cases, there are no specific blood tests that can tell us exactly what the causes of chronic pain are, even if the pain has been present for many years.

There is an exception, and this is a blood test specific to a disease called ankylosing spondylitis. This is a rare cause of chronic pain and stiffness in the neck and back, especially the lower back area.

However, there are no blood tests for a chronic pain condition such as fibromyalgia syndrome or FMS (see Useful

Information for more details on fibromyalgia). The doctor or specialist will make the diagnosis based on your symptoms and a physical examination.

Most people do not need blood tests because the doctor and/or physiotherapist can work from the history of your symptoms and the results of clinical examinations. So it's quite possible that you won't need any blood tests at all.

If you do have a test, you will be told that the result is either positive or negative:

A positive result may mean that:

- Further tests are needed. For example, if anaemia is present, then you may require further blood tests to determine the type of anaemia.
- No further blood tests are required.
- You need further investigation, like a CT scan or bone scan (see p. 57).

A negative result may mean that:

- You do not have the problem that has been tested for. The part of the body that the test checked is working normally. **This is the good news.**
- There are currently no blood tests that give a clear understanding of the reasons for the pain.
- The problems are functioning within pain system (see Chapter 2). In chronic pain, blood tests are often negative for this reason.

Here are some questions that you may want to ask your doctor:

- Do I need a blood test?
- If so, what is the test checking for?
- What does a negative result mean?
- What does a positive result mean?
- Could this help explain some of the reasons for my chronic pain?

Write down the answers in your notebook if possible.

X-rays and scans

Your doctor or specialist may recommend an x-ray, a bone scan, a CT scan or an MRI scan. There are difficulties about all these investigations because they do not always show clear, understandable reasons for the pain problem.

This may cause you to feel angry, worried and confused. However, it may help if you get more information by asking your doctor, or the specialist who ordered the test, some of these questions:

- What investigations are helpful for chronic pain?
- What do positive findings mean?
- What do negative findings mean?

Again, write the answers in your notebook if you can.

WHAT CAN X-RAYS TELL US?

X-rays of different parts of the body, such as the knee joint, back or neck, show bones, and their size, shape, surface, density and relationship to other bones and joints. This means that x-rays tell us about fractures, dislocations, and abnormally shaped bones. The term 'congenital' may be used to describe the way your bones or joints were originally formed before you were born.

X-rays can also show normal changes in the bone size, shape and joints which are related to growing older. Doctors, nurses, radiographers and physiotherapists may use many different terms for these normal, ageing changes, including spondylosis, old age, wear and tear, arthritis and osteoarthritis. Reports from radiologists may include comments about the bone size, shape of the joint, and the gap between the bones.

X-rays do not clearly show soft tissues like muscles, ligaments, tendons, nerves, discs and cartilage and do not show pain.

If you have an x-ray, you will be told that the result is normal, positive or negative:

DO I NEED AN X-RAY?

There are guidelines from the Royal College of Radiologists about which x-rays are the most helpful for which problems or symptoms. For example, the radiation dose in a CT scan is equal to 500 chest x-rays. Doctors use these guidelines, along with a history of symptoms and the results of clinical examinations, in order to decide whether or not a scan may help find any specific factors or causes for the pain. Doctors want to be sure that scans are going to be useful because they don't wish to expose people to increased levels of radiation from unnecessarily high numbers of x-rays or scans.

Doctors do not request x-rays of the spine very often. This is because spinal x-rays do not give much information about the reasons for chronic pain. They are useful when you have had an accident, to ensure that no fracture or dislocation has occurred. They are also helpful when symptoms, including pain, suggest infection or inflammation.

Scans

An MRI scan shows all the structures of the body very clearly. It shows skin, bones, soft tissues (including discs, large nerves, muscles, joints, cartilage, ligaments, blood vessels) and organs such as the heart, stomach, etc. It shows how parts of the body are changing because of age or disease. Repeated MRI scans can also show the speed of changes in the body tissues. These scans are taken at different angles, and sections through the body, to give a series of views. An MRI scan has no risk of radiation doses unlike CT Scans.

A CT scan also shows all the structures of the body clearly and is available in many places. It is used for specific problems in the brain, especially after head injury or strokes. CT scans are used when MRI scans are not available or for very specific assessment of spinal problems with myelography. On the whole, MRI scans are used, as they have less radiation risk. An MRI scan is the first-choice investigation for spinal cord symptoms or for chronic or persisting spinal pain problems.

A positive MRI or CT scan result may indicate that there is damage or pressure on nerve fibres.

A negative result can be helpful because it tells you that the structures scanned are normal. However, it does not tell you why you still have persistent or chronic pain. A negative result also means that it will do no harm to gradually increase physical activity despite pain. Chronic pain does not mean that you will harm or damage the pain areas or body tissues if you gradually increase your activities (see Chapters 8 and 9 for more on pacing skills and getting fitter).

BONE SCANS

There are two types of bone scan, a bone densitometry scan and an isotope bone scan.

A bone densitometry (or DEXA) scan finds out how dense your hip, wrist and spine bones are. The doctor will only request this test if you have significant risk factors for osteoporosis (see Useful Information for more on osteoporosis). Some of these factors are:

- An early (under 45) menopause
- Prolonged bed rest
- Being a smoker
- Having taken daily steroid drugs for many months or years

If you have no osteoporosis risk factors, there is no need to have this type of scan. If you are uncertain about whether or not a bone densitometry scan would be helpful in your case, talk to your doctor.

An isotope bone scan shows whether or not there is inflammation or increased bone cell activity. It helps find bone tumours that can occur within the bone tissue. It also helps find tumours that have spread from a cancer problem elsewhere in the body, e.g. from the lung, breast or kidney.

Waiting for tests and results

WHAT CAN I DO TO HELP MYSELF WHILE WAITING FOR TESTS AND THEIR RESULTS?

Keep as active as possible every day. This is important in order to prevent your body becoming unfit or out of condition. Lack of fitness can make pain symptoms worse. And pain researchers have discovered that we improve and heal while we move about. Long periods of rest do not help the body to manage persistent pain well.

There will be some days when the pain is severe. But, even on those days, it will do **no harm** to do parts of your activity programme or stretch-and-strengthen programme (see Chapter 9). If you are not certain what to do, or how to keep active, talk to your doctor or physiotherapist.

HOW CAN I COPE WITH WAITING FOR TEST RESULTS?

Waiting can be very difficult because worrying thoughts go through your mind. Some patients describe the waiting, and the lack of a definite diagnosis or cause, as 'soul-destroying'.

It is understandable that you and your family may become preoccupied with the pain because it can take over your everyday life. But the downside of this preoccupation is that the pain may then affect you and your activities even more. Generally, if a doctor or specialist has assessed you, they will order a test urgently if your symptoms and the results of a clinical examination suggest that something could be seriously wrong.

So, how do you cope with feelings of fear, anxiety and depression while waiting for test results? Here are some suggestions:

- You could read more about managing your moods in Chapter 14 of this book.
- You could write down your worries in your notebook and check them with your doctor, physiotherapist or hospital specialist.
- You could share your worries with someone you trust. Then ask yourself: did sharing your worries with this person help? If so, how?

- You could contact a self-help group (see the Useful Information section at the back of this book). Then ask yourself: did the group help? If so, how?

WHERE CAN I GO FOR MORE INFORMATION IF I DON'T FULLY UNDERSTAND THE ANSWERS TO MY QUESTIONS?

There are several options. You could:

- Ask the questions of your doctor or specialist again.
- Ask the questions of another member of your healthcare staff, such as your physiotherapist.
- Ask a self-help group for possible solutions (see the list of groups under Useful Information at the back of this book).
- Ask a patient liaison and advice service (PALS) to help. You may find PALS in your local hospital, where you had your tests or investigations.
- Check a reliable, helpful website (see the list of websites under Useful Information).

CHAPTER SUMMARY

- Blood tests are not usually helpful in finding a cause for chronic pain.
- X-rays and scans can sometimes help explain some of the reasons for chronic pain.
- Ask your doctor or specialist about the investigations and exactly what the results mean. This will reduce your anxiety, and help you manage life better, despite the pain.
- Remember to keep physically active while waiting for tests, investigations or results. It's important to be active, despite the pain, in order to prevent other pains developing from tight, inactive muscles and joints.

4

Understanding the roles of healthcare professionals

This chapter aims to help you understand more about:

- The roles of healthcare professionals, including physiotherapists, specialist pain nurses, pain specialists, psychologists and psychiatrists, in managing chronic pain
- How talking therapies, including Cognitive Behavioral Therapy, can help with chronic pain
- How pain management programmes work

Healthcare professionals

This chapter looks at the different healthcare professionals who may be involved in helping you to manage your pain better. Most of them will be highly trained in their own speciality and be very experienced in dealing with many aspects of pain.

Pain affects the whole person, so a 'multi-disciplinary' team with the expertise from different professions, working together can be very helpful. For example, a physiotherapist or a pain specialist doctor might provide acupuncture sessions, and the physiotherapist, psychologist or pain nurse might teach relaxation and pacing skills! They all help people with managing pain, and support their families and carers. Some other professionals may be involved and their roles are not described in detail here – for example, occupational therapists, art therapists, and doctors with different specialities.

What is the role of a physiotherapist?

A physiotherapist has specialist knowledge and experience of the musculoskeletal system, the pain system and how the nerves, bones, muscles and tendons, joints and ligaments work together. So physiotherapists understand the way the physical body works to allow movements such as walking, bending down or riding a bike. They can identify problems if you have difficulty making certain movements, or if you have pain or other symptoms such as lack of balance or recurring falls.

Physiotherapists have no training in using drugs to manage movement or pain problems. They do not prescribe any form of drug treatment.

If you have chronic pain, physiotherapists will know how it's likely to affect your physical activity and fitness levels in the long term. They will be able to show you a range of activities or exercises in order to gradually increase your stamina, strength and flexibility. They will also help you to learn useful skills, including how to:

- Pace your daily activities (see Chapter 8)
- Set goals in order to achieve things (see Chapter 6)
- Solve problems (see Chapter 10)
- Manage setbacks (see Chapter 16)
- Use relaxation techniques to manage your pain better (see Chapter 12)

How do physiotherapists work?

Firstly, they do a detailed assessment of your experience of pain. They will assess how it affects things like your daily activity, work, hobbies and sleep pattern. They may ask how and when the pain problem started, what investigations you have had, and what the results were.

Secondly, they do a physical examination, looking at how your musculoskeletal system is performing. They will assess your nerve function and mobility, muscle strength and length, the range of movement in your joints, and your reflexes and balance.

Thirdly, they tell you what is working normally and what parts of the musculoskeletal or movement systems require some intervention to help improve their function.

Fourthly, they may be able to help you plan ways to improve the way your body moves. This often means following a programme of different types of exercises, designed to improve flexibility, strength and stamina in your muscles, ligaments and tendons. These exercises can make it easier for you to carry out a range of physical activities in your everyday life, such as bending to put things away, or being able to walk further or have a better sex life. The aim is to help increase your self-confidence as well as your fitness.

Physiotherapists are trained to use specialist equipment and 'hands-on' manual therapy techniques. They are also often trained to use acupuncture and advise on the use of TENS (transcutaneous electrical nerve stimulation) machines. These machines are used for relief of pain. 'Transcutaneous' means 'through the skin', and the machine delivers small electrical pulses through electrodes placed on the skin. It can feel a little like 'pins and needles'. This sensation can change the way that pain signals are sent to the brain. That is, it can close the 'pain gate'. Around 50 per cent of people who try a TENS machine find that it can provide some pain relief while it is in use.

It may be helpful for you to see a private physiotherapist or for your GP to refer you to an NHS physiotherapy service. Before your first appointment, make a note of what daily physical activity problems you have because of your pain.

What is the role of a specialist pain nurse?

These are nurses who have special training in working with patients with chronic pain and their families. Specialist pain nurses often work with pain specialist doctors in hospitals, as well as with other members of specialist pain teams. These nurses can help you:

- Learn how to use pain-relief drugs more effectively, enabling you to manage your pain levels better. For example, if the pain specialist has given you drugs to try, the nurse may teach you how best to use them in your situation.
- Learn more about different ways of managing pain, especially during setbacks.
- Use other pain-reducing methods, such as TENS machines.
- Gain access to other specialist treatments for persistent pain, such as acupuncture.

What is the role of a pain specialist?

A pain specialist is normally a doctor who has trained as an anaesthetist and has developed additional skills in pain relief. Pain specialists usually work in a pain clinic and can offer different pain-reducing treatments. These treatments can include a range of drugs – in different forms, such as tablets, suppositories or skin patches.

Sometimes the pain specialist may suggest injections of pain-reducing drugs close to the nerves near the pain site. These treatments may help to relieve chronic pain for certain periods of time – perhaps weeks or months.

The pain specialist will sometimes carry out investigations to see if there are any specific causes for chronic pain. This may reveal the main factors contributing to the pain, and make it easier to plan different ways to reduce the pain levels. A pain specialist is more likely to carry out tests or investigations if you have additional symptoms, such as numbness, loss of feeling in the arms or legs, loss of bladder or bowel control, or great difficulty in walking.

If you see a pain specialist, you might want to ask what tests or investigations would be helpful.

What is the role of a psychologist?

Psychologists use a range of different talking therapies to gain an understanding of the way the mind and the body work together. These techniques enable them to help people who have chronic pain to understand how and why the pain affects their moods, thoughts and behavior (see the Person-Centred Model in Chapter 1, p. 26).

Psychologists can help people to:

- Understand their own reactions to upsetting or traumatic experiences in their lives, such as illness or family problems.
- Manage or cope with distressing mental health symptoms, which are relatively common. (As many as 1 in

4 people experience mental health problems at some point in their lives.)
- Cope better with emotional distress or mood problems, such as depression, anxiety, panic attacks, anger, eating disorders, post traumatic stress disorder, phobias and other mental health problems.
- Cope with the emotional upset and distress of having a physical illness, such as asthma, diabetes or heart failure.

Psychologists are not medically trained and do not prescribe drug treatments, such as tranquillizers or anti-depressants. They work with other healthcare professionals, such as hospital pain specialists or psychiatrists.

They use talking therapies and work with individual patients. They work with patients who have common problems, such as anxiety, worry or pain. They can also work with patients with chronic pain in a group.

HOW DO PSYCHOLOGISTS WORK?

Firstly, psychologists make an individual assessment and listen to your experiences. They are skilled in asking questions to help you understand:

- Your difficulties with pain now.
- How much the pain affects your thinking, your moods, and things you do or don't do.
- How much the pain has changed you as a person.
- How you cope and struggle with the pain.

Secondly, they help you understand that chronic pain can sometimes overwhelm your ability to cope. If this happens, you may become depressed or have other mood changes.

Thirdly, they help you realize that there are many strategies you can use to gain more confidence in managing and living with your pain. These may include:

- Ways of managing your own fear, frustration, anger, guilt and other moods or unhelpful thoughts linked to the pain.
- Relaxation skills, or problem-solving or other techniques.
- Ways to cope with other people's reactions to your pain and to be more assertive.
- Ways to cope with the losses in your life because of your pain.

Your GP or hospital specialist may refer you to a psychologist because some of your symptoms are affecting your daily life. For example, you might be worrying a lot, having difficulty sleeping, getting very irritated and angry, bursting into tears a lot more than usual, and perhaps avoiding going out and meeting people.

They will first refer you for an assessment, because time is needed to talk and listen, to make sense of difficulties and find helpful ways of coping. Your GP or hospital specialist may feel that it would be helpful to focus on what can be changed, because of the effect of the pain on you as a person.

If you are referred to a psychologist, it does not mean that the pain is 'all in the mind'.

It does mean that your pain is real and its effect on your life can sometimes be very hurtful, distressing and limiting.

Any continual or repeated health problem (such as kidney failure, severe angina, colitis or epilepsy) will affect a person every day and will therefore affect their moods, their thinking and what they do.

Hospital specialists are not trained in psychology or psychiatry. They only have specialist experience in one area of the physical body. They will refer you to another healthcare practitioner, such as a psychologist, for an assessment of the pain and its effect on you as a person.

What is the role of a psychiatrist?

Psychiatrists are medically qualified doctors who specialize in mental health problems such as severe depression or anxiety or other mental health problems such as schizophrenia. In chronic pain psychiatrists can assess a person's difficulties and suggest therapies or treatments to help severe depression, anxiety, psychotic conditions or disorders such as obsessive compulsive disorder.

These treatments may include prescribing different drugs to help change moods and conditions. They may also involve referral to a team of mental health professionals who will use a range of talking therapies in order to offer support while the severity of the depression or condition changes for the better.

Talking therapies

Chronic pain may have an impact on your moods, your life at home or at work, your relationships with your family, your partner, even your doctor. It can be a very distressing and miserable experience, making you feel quite alone and different from other people. You may feel that you have lost a great deal – from fitness to friends to employment. For all these reasons, it can be very helpful to talk about the way the pain is affecting you as a person.

Talking therapies can help you share the ways in which the pain has changed your thoughts, moods and daily life. They can also help you talk through what you feel you have lost in different parts of your life. This can enable you to find ways of coping with the pain and to think about how things could change.

Cognitive Behavioral Therapy

Cognitive Behavioral Therapy (or CBT) is a talking therapy that can help you understand the links between the five parts of yourself. These five parts, described in the Person-Centred Model in Chapter 1, are:

- Body symptoms, such as pain
- Thoughts
- Moods or emotions
- Actions or behaviors
- What is happening in your life situation

In CBT, you work with a therapist who helps you learn more about dealing with moods, such as depression or anxiety. The therapist also shows you different ways to cope with unhelpful thinking patterns and actions.

Research has shown that CBT can be helpful in treating many different mental health problems, including depression, anxiety, panic attacks and post-traumatic stress disorder. CBT can also be used to treat physical health problems, such as chronic pain, and other chronic illnesses, such as heart failure. This is because physical health problems can affect people's moods and their lives in so many difficult and distressing ways. CBT therapists can help by showing people how to recognize and change unhelpful ways of thinking and behaving. This allows them to be less affected by unhelpful moods and to enjoy life more, even if they still have pain.

Pain management programmes

A pain management programme aims to help people with persistent pain learn skills to cope with life better, despite the pain problems. On a pain management programme, people learn more about:

- Pain systems and how they work in the body (see Chapter 2)
- Medicines and better ways to manage them (see Chapter 5)
- Becoming fitter and more active, and using stretching and strengthening exercises to regain or increase fitness (see Chapter 9)
- Using pacing of activities to help reduce severe pain levels (see Chapter 8)
- Setting goals (see Chapter 6)
- Solving problems (see Chapter 10)
- Rewarding yourself (see Chapter 7)
- Maintaining positive changes gained through being fitter and pacing activities (see Chapter 16)
- Talking through difficulties with others, especially partners and family (see Chapter 13)
- Managing moods, such as depression, anger and worry or anxiety (see Chapter 14)
- Using relaxation skills, such as deep breathing or relaxing imagery or sounds, or meditation (see Chapter 12)

The programme will often involve working with other pain sufferers in a group, to learn these skills with support from each other. Group leaders work together as a healthcare team, often called a pain management or pain rehabilitation team. The programme may run over several weeks, and the number and length of sessions can vary between different pain management teams. It is a bit like going on a part-time course to learn to manage your pain better. Many people with chronic pain have found these programmes very helpful.

ONE GRADUATE OF A PAIN MANAGEMENT PROGRAMME SAID:

I was able to move forward and learn to cope and accept my pain. The group support from other pain sufferers, who knew what it was like to deal with the pain, made a big difference. They really understood and offered different ways and ideas to deal with problems. It helped my family, as they realized that more activities were possible if I paced myself better. My frustration lessened and I was able to laugh again a bit more often.

After a pain management programme, you might expect to be able to:

- Take up new activities
- Start a study or computer course
- Start voluntary work for a few hours each week
- Return to work, often through special schemes that are available locally

WOULD A PAIN MANAGEMENT PROGRAMME HELP ME?

Asking yourself some questions may help you decide:

- Would I like to be more active or become fitter?
- Do I have problems pacing my day-to-day activities?
- Do I feel stiff and tense in different parts of my body?
- Do I have mood changes, such as depression, anger, anxiety or stress, because of the pain?
- Would it help to know more about pain systems in the body?
- Do I want to use my pain-relief medicines better or reduce them?
- Would I value working in a group with other pain sufferers to learn how to manage better?

If you answered 'Yes' to two or more of the above questions, then a pain management programme may well be helpful. In order to be referred on to a pain management programme, you will need an assessment. If you already have contact with a health professional who specializes in pain, the first step would be to discuss local pain management programmes with them. Otherwise, you can begin by discussing your needs with your GP or family doctor and ask for a referral to a pain management team.

Alternatively, you could make contact with local self-help pain management groups or access information from the web-sites in the Useful Information section at the back of this book.

CHAPTER SUMMARY

- Pain can affect all five parts of a person: their life situation, their moods, their thinking, their behavior and their body symptoms.
- A range of different healthcare professionals can offer advice and support to help people manage life better despite the pain.
- Talking therapies can offer a chance to talk through life changes resulting from pain as well as ways of coping with pain and its effects on moods, thoughts, actions and life situation.
- Pain management programmes are a useful way to learn more about chronic pain and how to cope better. These programmes involve working with a group of pain sufferers to gain these skills. Support is provided by other pain sufferers in the group and by healthcare staff.

5

Understanding medicines and using them better

This chapter aims to help you understand:

- What types of medicines are used to manage chronic pain
- How are medicines used
- What the problems are with medicines
- How to make better use of medicines
- How to reduce or stop your use of medicines

If you are taking medicines for pain, it may be useful to ask yourself the following questions:

- How long have you used your pain-relief medicines?
- Have they helped reduce your pain?
- Have you any side-effects, problems or concerns about your medicines?
- Do you ever try to cope without them?

This chapter gives you guidance on using your medicines in helpful ways and making decisions about changes with your doctor at any stage. The chapter mentions the most common medicines used to reduce pain and does not include all the possible ones that manage pain.

What types of medicines are used to manage chronic pain?

There are four main types of medicines that are used to manage pain: analgesics (including opioids), anti-inflammatories, anti-depressants and anti-convulsants.

ANALGESICS

Analgesics, like paracetamol, codeine, dihydrocodeine, buprenorphine, tramadol, morphine, fentanyl, oxycodone are often called 'painkillers'.

Opioids, like codeine, dihydrocodeine and morphine, are chemical or drug forms of pain relief susbstances found in opium poppy seeds. There are several newer opioid drugs, like tramadol, fentanyl and buprenorphine.

The body also makes its own opioid-like substances, called endorphins, which can help reduce the pain experience. Exercise and physical activity or relaxation can increase endorphins, and raised endorphins create a feeling of happiness or euphoria, sometimes known as a 'runner's high'. All these opioid drugs mimic the action of the endorphins' pain relief effects. They attach to the opioid receptors in the brain and spinal cord to reduce pain signals in the pain systems.

The word 'painkiller' suggests that analgesics relieve pain completely. However, most people with chronic pain find that these drugs can be used to help reduce or control the pain, but do not relieve it totally.

Common side-effects of analgesics include: constipation, feeling sick, itching, dizziness, loss of concentration, forgetfulness, dry mouth, mood changes, such as depression, and sleep problems, sometimes including dreams or nightmares.

ANTI-INFLAMMATORIES

Anti-inflammatories reduce inflammation and pain, e.g.:

- In acute injuries, like a twisted ankle
- Around joints, for example in osteoarthritis or rheumatoid arthritis
- In sore throats
- After the removal of a tooth

Inflammation shows as swelling or redness of the affected area and this causes pain. Inflammation is caused by a release of many helpful chemicals in the injured or infected area. These chemicals send pain messages through the nerve endings in the area to the brain's pain centres. The same chemicals help the body to limit any further damage from the injury and start the healing process. They also work with the body's immune system to control infection.

Some frequently used anti-inflammatory drugs include: ibuprofen (Brufen), indomethacin (Indocid) and diclofenac (Voltarol). These drugs are known as non-steroidal anti-inflammatory drugs.

Common side-effects of anti-inflammatory drugs include: skin rashes, indigestion, and bleeding from the gut, stomach or bowel. They can sometimes worsen asthma symptoms.

ANTI-DEPRESSANTS

Anti-depressants or tricyclic anti-depressants, such as amitriptyline, imipramine or dothiepin, are usually used in treating depression. Research has shown them to be also very useful in helping to reduce chronic pain and sleep problems (both helping getting off to sleep and reducing waking from sleep due to pain). For example, with amitriptyline, the dose used to manage chronic pain is usually quite small, between 5 mg and 25 mg. In depression, the dose used is up to ten times larger, between 100 and 200 mg.

Common side-effects of these anti-depressants include: constipation, dry mouth, drowsiness, abdominal pain due to colic or constipation, dizziness, blurred vision and poor concentration.

ANTI-CONVULSANTS

Anti-convulsants, such as carbamazepine and gabapentin, are used for pain. They are also used to treat epilepsy. They can reduce pain coming from nerve fibres, called neuropathic pain. Research shows it can help reduce pain in diabetes neuropathy and is sometimes helpful in trigeminal neuralgia or after shingles (post herpetic neuralgia).

Common side-effects of anti-convulsants include: drowsiness, rashes, nausea and vomiting, dizziness, and unsteadiness or balance difficulties.

Note: Current medical opinion states that tranquillizers, or muscle and mind relaxants, such as diazepam (Valium) and lorazepam (Ativan), which are sometimes used to control convulsions, have no use in acute back pain management. This would suggest that they have no use in treating any kind of chronic pain. Dependence can be a **real** problem with these drugs. If they have been used for months or years, careful support from a healthcare practitioner is essential in order to help people reduce their dose.

How are medicines used?

Analgesics

Currently the World Health Organisation (WHO) suggests that analgesics are used in a series of three steps depending on the level of pain. Pain levels are rated from 0 (no pain) to 10 (worst pain ever).

WHO STEP ONE:

For mild pain level (less than 4):
Non-opioid analgesics, e.g. paracetamol or aspirin
Anti-inflammatories, e.g. ibuprofen or diclofenac

WHO STEP TWO:

For moderate pain level (4–7):
Weak opioid drugs, e.g.
Codeine phosphate (doses vary, e.g. 15 mg, 30 mg, 60 mg)
Codydramol = Paracetamol 500 mg + dihydrocodeine 10 mg
Co-Codamol = Paracetamol 500 mg + codeine 8 mg or 30 mg
Dihydrocodeine 30 mg or slow-release forms
Tramadol 50–100 mg or slow-release forms

WHO STEP THREE:

Severe pain level (7–10):
Strong opioid drugs, e.g. Morphine, which can be taken in different ways, such as liquid oral morphine sulphate, or

in long-acting preparations like MST (doses vary, e.g. 10 mg, 30 mg, 60 mg, 100 mg), or even as suppositories.

Buprenorphine, oxycodone and fentanyl are other opioid drugs that can be taken for severe pain.

All these opioid drugs can cause dependence.

Problems with medicines

WHY DON'T MEDICINES ALWAYS REDUCE CHRONIC PAIN?

Deciding which analgesic to use for pain can be a difficult process of trial and error. Doctors often start with mild analgesics, such as paracetamol or co-codamol, and may try to match the pain level with the right type and dose of a drug.

Analgesics work well for acute pain problems, where there is an injury or inflammation, like a sprained wrist or a headache. They also relieve the pain in heart attacks, fractures, after operations, and in burns and inflammations such as throat infections.

However, people with chronic pain often find that analgesics are not very useful in reducing their pain. This is because the chronic pain system works very differently from the acute pain system (see Chapter 2). These are some of the problems that can occur in the chronic pain system:

- When the pain system is on 'high alert', the pain receptors in the pain areas act like over-sensitive burglar alarm sensors. They may set off the 'alarm' even when there is no 'burglar'.
- The pain nerves (called C fibres) that take signals to and from the pain site in the body to the pain centres

in the brain, are sometimes faulty. The effect is rather like what happens when all the traffic lights are faulty and out of sequence at a busy crossroads.

- The pain centres in the brain try to make sense of all the different types of signals coming from many areas in the body and the brain. Sometimes they become confused and give out a 'pain alert' when it is not needed. So again an alarm is set off when there is no 'burglar'.

These difficulties in the pain system seem to cause and maintain pain themselves. Other factors, such as being depressed or anxious, being unfit, or being tense and under strain, also contribute to chronic pain. Researchers are trying to understand these chronic pain system difficulties better, in order to find better ways to relieve this type of pain in the future.

WHAT IS TOLERANCE?

People may develop tolerance to many medicines, including analgesics, when they take them for many weeks or months. Tolerance means that the medicine becomes less effective at reducing the pain over time (usually a matter of weeks). The dose of the medicine has to be increased in order to get the *same* amount of pain reduction. This leads to bigger doses of the medicine being taken and many more side-effects.

WHAT IS DEPENDENCE?

Medicine dependence means addiction, and it mainly happens when medicines are misused. For instance, people might take increasing doses without assessing whether they are really reducing their pain levels. Dependence can occur within a few days or weeks of use. And people may get withdrawal symptoms, such as a dry mouth, shaking, itching and feeling sick, when they reduce or stop the medication.

WHAT ARE THE SIDE-EFFECTS OF MEDICINES?

All medicines have side-effects. Here are the most common ones:

- Dependency
- Constipation
- Nausea and vomiting
- Indigestion
- Dry mouth
- Dizziness
- Tiredness
- Poor concentration
- Mood changes or mood swings, e.g. depression, feeling anxious
- Poor memory, forgetful
- Feeling of detachment – 'not really with it'
- Hallucinations
- Dreams/nightmares

Any others? (List them in your notebook.)

HOW DO MEDICINES REACT WITH OTHER MEDICINES?

Medicinies can have effects on other medicines and the way they work in the body. This is called a drug interaction and it can happen with any of the medicines taken for pain. For instance:

- Tramadol and amitriptyline, or other anti-depressants, can increase drowsiness.
- Different analgesics can change the effect of carbamazepine. Some reduce its effect and others increase it.
- Some pain-relief medicines will affect medicines used for other conditions such as heart disease.

It is important to check with your doctor, pain specialist or pharmacist whether your medicines interact or can have an antagonistic effect with each other.

WHAT ABOUT ALLERGIC REACTIONS TO MEDICINES?

Some people are allergic to certain medicines and may experience additional problems, such as rashes, fevers and other symptoms. It's hard to predict who is going to have an allergic reaction to a pain-relief medicine but it is more likely to happen in people who have allergies to other medicines. If you are concerned about this problem, talk to your doctor.

Making better use of medicines

Start by checking to see which types of medicines you are using. Which of these do you take at present?

Analgesics:
Paracetamol + / − Codeine
Codeine
Dihydrocodeine
Tramadol
Morphine

Oxycodone
Buprenorphine
Fentanyl
Other?

Anti-inflammatories:
Ibuprofen
Diclofenac
Indomethacin
Other?

Anti-depressants:
Amitriptyline
Dothiepin
Imipramine
Other?

Anti-convulsants:
Carbamazepine
Gabapentin
Lamotrigine
Other?

Creams or gels:
Capsaicin cream
Diclofenac gel
Other?

Make a list in your notebook of all the medicines, including remedies, that you take at present.

Overall, what level of relief do you get from your medicines on a typical day?

Put a mark **X** on the line below to indicate how much relief on average you get from using your pain-relief medicines:

1	2	3	4	5	6	7	8	9	10
No pain relief									Pain-free

Four suggestions for using medications more helpfully

At present, you may find yourself taking a lot of different tablets to reduce pain. This may mean that you are taking too many, too often and perhaps experiencing side-effects or interactions with other medicines. If you think this is happening, try Suggestion A (below), using a medicine diary. (If you are concerned or uncertain about your pain-relief medicine, then discuss the problem with your doctor or specialist pain nurse first.)

Medicine is just one way of controlling persistent pain. Staying or getting active, stretching and exercising, relaxation skills, pleasurable activities, learning distraction techniques and even staying or returning to work can also contribute to better pain control.

SUGGESTION A

Keeping a diary for three to four days will enable you to see your pain patterns during the day and at night-time. The diary will help you monitor your use of medication, in different situations and moods and with different pain levels.

MEDICINES USE DIARY

Situation		Pain level (0 = no pain 10 = worst pain ever)	Type of medication and how many taken
Razia Who am I with? What am I doing? When? Where? (place) What mood at the time?	Example: With son Washing dishes 2 p.m. At home Cross and worried	8	Ibuprofen 400 mg Paracetamol × 2
What am I doing? When? Where? (place) What mood at the time? Who am I with?			
What am I doing? When? Where? (place) What mood at the time?			
What am I doing? When? Where? (place) What mood at the time?			
What am I doing? When? Where? (place) What mood at the time?			
What am I doing? When? Where? (place) What mood at the time?			

There is a spare Medicines Use Diary sheet, if you need it, at the back of the book (see p. 296).

SUGGESTION B

How severe does the pain get before you take or change your medication?

Put a mark **X** on the line below to indicate how severe the pain is:

1	2	3	4	5	6	7	8	9	10
No pain							Worst imaginable pain		

Waiting until pain levels are very high (say 7–10) is usually an unhelpful way to use medicines. This is called 'the hanging on' trap or the 'wait and see' trap, because the high pain level cannot easily be reduced with mild or moderate analgesics. Catching it sooner can work better – so try taking your pain-relieving medicines as pain levels start to rise. This may mean that you can carry on with your daily routine with less pain.

Try to predict when your pain level is likely to increase during your daytime or night-time activities. For example, pain levels can rise after physical activities or sometimes when you are stressed or angry. Then start analgesics as the pain levels start to rise.

Suggestions B and C both use the Gate Control system (see pp. 45–7) to help close the pain gate to pain messages.

SUGGESTION C

This method helps you gain better pain control by taking medicines at regular times or by the clock, not just by the pain level.

First ask yourself the following questions:

1 Do you take several types of medicines at the same time to give pain relief?
2 If the pain level stays high for two/three hours after taking pain medicine, what do you do next?

   (a) Do you, for example, take more tablets than you should to deal with the high pain levels?
   (b) Do you take tablets earlier than the next dose time to deal with the high pain levels?
   (c) Do you try something else, such as a hot bath or a distracting activity such as a puzzle game or deep-breathing relaxation?

Write what you do now in your notebook or in your Medicines Use Diary.

Taking too many types of medicines or too many tablets within two or three hours can cause side-effects or drug reactions and the pain levels may still be high.

It may help to try and take medicine at regular times. This can be four-hourly for medicines like paracetamol (though no more than eight tablets in 24 hours), or for stronger medicines like codeine, dihyrocodeine or opioids such as oral morphine. It can be ten- to twelve-hourly if using slow-release forms of medicine like dihyrocodeine, morphine, tramadol or oxycodone. Continue taking your medicine at regular times when the pain is at high levels. If you have 'breakthrough pain' (increased pain levels before your next dose is due), then talk to your doctor or pain specialist nurse to get help with this situation.

It may also help to match the level of pain with the strength of the medicine (see the WHO Steps One, Two and Three on p. 78). Talk to your doctor or specialist pain nurse about the use of stronger medicine for your specific situation.

Look at Steve's Medicine and Pain Level Diary (opposite) when he was trying oral morphine solution to reduce his pain.

It can help to use a Medicine and Pain Level Diary. This allows you to record pain levels every three or four hours through the day and night and the medicines you take and when you use them. You and your doctor or pain specialist nurse can use this to see when the medications help reduce the pain. It will also enable your doctor or pain specialist nurse to see when there is breakthrough pain. They can then suggest different strengths or types of drugs to help improve pain relief. Using strong medicines, like morphine or oxycodone, for severe pain in this way is safe and rarely causes dependence or addiction. Many people stay on morphine, oxycodone or fentanyl (a medication used in patches that are stuck on to the skin) safely for years to help reduce and manage their pain.

SUGGESTION D

This involves reducing the medicines you take or stopping them over time (see below).

Have you ever thought about stopping or reducing your medications?

If 'Yes', is this because:

- You are concerned about becoming dependent?
- Side-effects are a problem?
- You are concerned about becoming drug-tolerant?
- You are concerned for other reasons? If so, what are they?

TABLE 5.1: STEVE'S MEDICINE AND PAIN LEVEL DIARY			
Day	Pain level (0 = no pain; 10 = worst ever pain)	Dose and time of medicines	Comments/situation
Monday	8–9	15 ml 8.55 a.m.	Only woke once!!
Tuesday	3	15 ml 4.30 a.m.	Felt low
Tuesday	4	15 ml 12.55 p.m.	Out walking
Tuesday	5–6	15 ml 4.55 p.m.	
Tuesday	4	15 ml 9.10 p.m.	2 paracetamol at bedtime
Tuesday	5	15 ml 4.30 a.m.	Woke, morphine. Helped sleep in until 8 a.m.
Wednesday	7	15 ml 9.05 a.m.	
Wednesday	4	15 ml 1.05 p.m.	Driving a lot; took paracetamol × 2 tablets

Stopping or reducing your medicines

For people with chronic pain, some doctors and specialist pain nurses suggest that stopping or reducing the number or types of medicines can be a helpful choice. This is especially true when there are many problems, or the side-effects are very distressing or severe. For instance, some people find that their pain-relief medicine make them very drowsy, moody and unable to concentrate.

If you decide that you want to stop or reduce your medicine, you first need to think about whether or not they help you to manage your chronic pain at present.

Start by making a list of the advantages and disadvantages of continuing to take medicine for your pain problem. You can use the following questions to help you:

1 How much do your medicines relieve your pain? Tick your answer.

0—10—20—30—40—50—60—70—80—90—100%
No pain relief   Pain-free

2 Do you have side-effects with your current medicines? Tick those that apply.

- ❑ Concentration difficulties
- ❑ Constipation
- ❑ Sickness
- ❑ Dizziness
- ❑ Hallucinations
- ❑ Rashes
- ❑ Blurred vision
- ❑ Dry mouth
- ❑ Mood changes
- ❑ Sexual difficulties
- ❑ Other (write them down)

3 Does the pain-relief effect reduce, despite increasing the dose regularly?
4 Do you get any dependence symptoms? Tick those that apply.

- ❑ Shaking
- ❑ Tremors
- ❑ Nausea/vomiting
- ❑ Diarrhoea
- ❑ Itching

5 Do drugs help in a setback with high pain levels?
6 Do they help you feel good about yourself?
7 Do they help you get a good night's sleep?
8 Do they help you to keep doing the things that are important to you?

Think about your answers. Think about how much relief you get with your medicines, and how many side-effects or dependence symptoms. Do they help you? Or do they get in the way of doing all the things that are important to you?

Now write down in your notebook, in two columns, the advantages and disadvantages of continuing medicines for your pain problem.

Looking through this list, do the benefits of medicines on balance outweigh the disadvantages? If so, this would suggest that it is worth continuing to use them.

If there are more disadvantages than advantages, then you need to think over two options:

- reducing the type and number of medicines
- gradually stopping the medicines

You may want to discuss these options with your doctor or pain specialist team.

OPTION ONE

Option One involves reducing your medicines slowly over time, rather than stopping them all at once. There are a couple of important rules when following this option:

- Reduce your dose by one tablet every two or three days, choosing a time when your pain level is low.
- Reduce one type of medicine at a time.

This option is likely to lead to success. Up to 70 per cent of patients are able to cut down on the types of medicines or numbers of tablets, and some eventually stop their medicines completely.

If you are uncertain about the best way to reduce or stop your medicines, discuss the options with your doctor or pain specialist.

You can also use skills such as pacing (see Chapter 8), stretches and relaxation (see Chapter 12), and anger management (see Chapter 14) to help cope with the pain as you reduce your drugs.

OPTION TWO

It is possible to stop all pain-relief drugs at once. However, it can make you feel unwell and the pain can really increase. Gradual reduction is sensible, until you have stopped all your pain-relief medicine, ie. option one.

Note: If you take medicines for any other problem, such as diabetes or high blood pressure, do **not** reduce or stop them. Check with your doctor, pain specialist or pharmacist if you are uncertain at any stage as to what to do about your medication.

When you see your doctor or pharmacist, take a list of all the medicines you take and write down the questions you want to ask.

For instance, it may help to ask:

- What does this medicine do?
- How long will I need to take it?
- How and when should I take it?
- Are there any drugs, foods, drinks or activities I should avoid or change when taking this medicine?

- What are the common side-effects and what should I do if I get them?
- Other questions or notes?

CHAPTER SUMMARY

- Chronic pain can sometimes be helped by analgesics and other medicines, such as amitriptyline. It is a process of trial and error to see if drugs can help.
- Matching pain levels to the strength of the analgesic can be helpful to reduce pain. However, stronger analgesics may give more side-effects. The WHO ladder for analgesics can help guide medicine use, matching the right medicine to a particular pain level.
- Predicting pain increases, and using drugs before high pain levels set in, can help you control pain. Filling in a Medicine Use Diary can enable you to understand your pain patterns and use medicines better. The diary can also give your doctor/pain specialist useful information on the helpful and unhelpful effects of medicines.
- Reducing the number of different medications reduces side-effects. Stopping medicines can be very helpful when there are many problems with them, their side-effects or dependence symptoms.
- It helps to use pacing, relaxation and other skills to manage pain levels as you make changes with your medicines.
- Talk to your doctor or pain specialist team if you need help to make changes.

PART TWO

Overcoming Chronic Pain

Introduction

Chronic pain can be disabling, distressing and frustrating for many people, partly because it does not respond well to medical treatments. It is a condition that affects the person with pain as well as their family, friends and work colleagues.

Many people find themselves in a cycle of pain and distress, which has an impact on several aspects of everyday life:

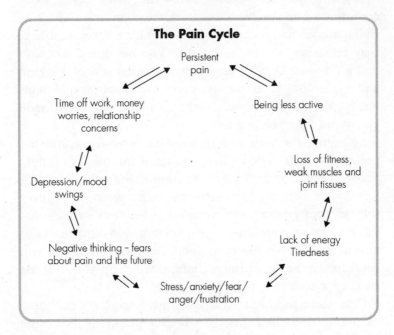

The Pain Cycle

Persistent pain

Time off work, money worries, relationship concerns

Being less active

Loss of fitness, weak muscles and joint tissues

Depression/mood swings

Lack of energy Tiredness

Negative thinking – fears about pain and the future

Stress/anxiety/fear/ anger/frustration

The chapters in Part Two offer information and practical strategies to help you cope better, one day at a time, despite ongoing pain. You can use the Guide to Overcoming Chronic Pain (see p. 10) to guide your choice of which areas to focus on.

Cognitive behavioral approaches can help change the way you view the impact of pain on your life and your future. For example, learning to set specific, achievable goals can help you to tackle activities more successfully. Learning how to pace daily activities and using relaxation skills will allow you to increase what you can do in a manageable way. Getting fitter can affect how you think about yourself, your life and future, improve your moods and the impact of the pain, enabling you to believe that it is possible to achieve many of your current goals.

Learning problem-solving skills can mean being more confident when you hit obstacles. Understanding and identifying mood changes and negative thinking styles, and how they relate to your pain, can help you manage depression and low mood. Developing a more balanced way of thinking and challenging unhelpful thoughts can enable you to manage negative thought cycles that might otherwise have made you avoid doing certain things.

Changing the way you manage anxiety, anger and depression can mean being less emotional and more confident about getting on with your life despite the pain. Learning techniques to count your successes, such as using positive self-talk and giving yourself rewards for your own efforts, can help boost your self-esteem. Relationship difficulties can also be eased by being clear about the type of support you need from others. All these changes will help you to focus more on achievements and less on pain.

Relaxation techniques can help give most people some 'time out' or skills to use in stressful situations. For some people, relaxation in itself can give some relief from pain. Accepting that long-lasting pain is part of your life can be difficult and frustrating and may take some time. Using acceptance skills to manage the things you can't change can lead to a sense of contentment. It can also open awareness of new possibilities in life and lead to more confidence in handling the limitations the pain brings.

Experimenting with all these different skills in different ways, steadily and realistically, may enable you to return to hobbies, study or full-time or part-time work.

6

Setting goals

This chapter aims to help you understand more about:

- What goals are
- How to set goals
- How to achieve the goals you have planned

What are goals?

Goals are plans of activities or things that you wish to achieve for yourself or with others, despite having chronic pain. Goal setting is a very useful skill to help you live with chronic pain. You can set both short-term and long-term goals – to suit your needs. Goal setting helps you focus on important activities, achieve success and increase your self-confidence.

For example, to become more physically active, you might set yourself the goal of swimming 12 lengths of the local pool twice a week over a two-month period. Or, if you want to mix with people more, you might set a goal of having a family meal out or a day shopping with friends once a month.

Goals are a helpful way of watching and recording your progress. They enable you to see and believe that change is possible in a range of activities, despite the pain. Sometimes, if you are suffering from chronic pain, activities take longer and require more planning. It doesn't mean they are impossible. Setting goals puts you back in the driving seat and helps you regain control in many different areas of your life.

Informal and formal goals

Setting goals, when you have no pain, is a normal day-to-day activity. You may not even be aware of setting goals. For instance, you may think: 'I'll do this today, then I will go there . . . and then I can do that.'

Think about the goals that you frequently and informally set yourself. For example, 'I'll go and do some weeding in the garden' or 'I'll just clean the bedroom' or 'I'll paint the kitchen door' are all goals stated in an informal way.

In chronic pain it can be helpful to set goals in a formal way in order to achieve particular activities or tasks. Planning goals formally may be new to you, and it may take a little practice until you feel confident about setting them regularly.

What are SMART goals?

Your goals also need to be **SMART**, meaning that they should be:

- Specific
- Measurable
- Achievable
- Realistic
- Timed

Using SMART to set your goals will give you a clear view of what you want to achieve by a set time. It will help you plan how you get there. And it will help others to see what you hope to achieve with your goals. All these factors will increase your chances of success.

WHAT DO THESE FACTORS REALLY MEAN?

Specific: Be clear about what you actually want to do. For instance, 'Be more active' isn't that clear. But 'Walk more' tells you and others exactly what you want to do.

Measurable: Set a measurable goal. For instance 'Walking three times ($3 \times$) per week for half an hour' tells you and others when you have reached your goal.

Achievable: This may be tricky. Think about what you are capable of doing now. Then try to picture what you think you can achieve within your time period, for example eight weeks.

Realistic: Be honest and reasonable with yourself. For instance, climbing a 3000-foot mountain in the Lake District may not be realistic, in 3 months' time. However, it may be a realistic long-term goal for 12 months' time.

Timed: Decide how much time you are going to give yourself in order to achieve your goal. It may be a few weeks, which would be a **short-term goal**. Several months or even years would be a **long-term goal**.

Setting goals

People often say, 'There are so many things that I want to achieve, I don't know where to start.' It may help to divide your goals up into areas, as in the examples opposite:

Have a look at these examples and then, for each area, decide on a goal for yourself:

I want to achieve . . . by the end of . . . weeks.

TABLE 6.1: SETTING GOALS	
Area	Example
Social activities	Going out for a meal
Work	Staying at or returning to work, training, learning new skills
Hobbies	Gardening, fishing, decorating, bowling
Household tasks	Vacuuming, ironing, making the beds, cooking meals
Increasing physical activity	Doing some stretches and exercises, being up and about more
Caring for myself	Getting dressed on my own, sewing on buttons, having a bath

Write down at least three goals in your notebook.

Then, for each goal, write down all the skills and information you need to help you achieve that goal.

It may be helpful to look at some examples of people from the Case Histories you read earlier (see pp. 11–19). For instance, **Razia** wants to achieve a physical activity goal. She wants to be able to swim twice per week for 30 minutes. And she wants to achieve her goal in eight weeks.

What skills and information does Razia need to achieve her goal? She might need to:

- Find out the opening times of the local pool and how much it costs to swim
- Find out the bus route and timetable
- Buy or borrow some swimming goggles
- Improve the flexibility, strength and stamina in her arm and neck muscles (see Chapter 9)

- Practise deep breathing and relaxation skills (see Chapter 12)
- Work on her pacing skills (see Chapter 8)
- Learn how to reward herself for making progress (see Chapter 7)

You may have thought of other things you need to know or do to achieve your goals. In your notebook, write the key pieces of information and skills that you need for one of your goals.

Using a goal ladder

A useful total time period to set for a goal is six to eight weeks. Then you can divide your goal into six or eight smaller short-term goals. Write one small goal next to each step on the ladder. Each step is a week.

You can use the ladder on p. 107 for each of your goals. The ladder gives you your plan, week by week, helping you reach a specific goal.

For example, look at Steve's goal ladder for an eight-week period. Steve's goal aims to gradually build up his skills and fitness levels, working towards his goal to wash his car by hand.

Steve knows that he may have setbacks and barriers to his progress during the eight weeks. So he needs to plan for these setbacks and be prepared to review his plan if he has problems. Taking one step at a time increases his chances of being successful.

STEVE'S GOAL LADDER

My goal is to wash the car by hand
Time: 8 weeks

Week	Activities to help me achieve my goal	Things that *helped* my progress	Things that *blocked* my progress
Start:	Daily walk × 10 mins.		
Week 1	Relaxation and breathing after walk.		
Week 2	Daily walk × 15 mins. Stretches × 2/day. Relaxation and breathing. Fill the bucket, take to drive.	Noticed my pacing was helping progress.	Handle broken, needed a new bucket.
Week 4	Daily walk × 25 mins. Stretches × 2/day. Muscle relaxation. Fill the bucket, lift, walk to the car, wash car bonnet.	Found using the music relaxation tape really helpful when washing the bonnet.	Car needed servicing.
Week 5	Daily walk × 30 mins. Stretches × 2/day. Relaxed muscles. ¾ fill the bucket, walk to the car, wash car bonnet and 2 doors.	Rewarded myself with a beer!	Bad pain week – a setback.
Week 8	Daily walk × 30 mins. Stretches × 2/day. Relaxation and imagery. ¾ fill the bucket with water, walk to the car, wash car bonnet and 2 doors and roof.	Nicole my partner made a cup of tea and said 'What a good achievement'. Lucky it's a two-door car!	

EXAMPLE: RAZIA'S GOAL LADDER FOR A SHORT-TERM GOAL

My short-term goal is: to be able to cook a meal at the weekends for family and friends

Time: 3 weeks

Week	Activities to help me achieve my goal	Things that *helped* my progress	Things that *blocked* my progress
Start Week 1	Find out what cooking equipment I need. Make a list of what need to use. Arrange to have the oven fixed. Decide who and how many to invite, arrange a date with them. Check if any foods not suitable or dislike.	Contact people by phone in early evening.	Oven is broken again. Too many people want to come! Limit to 8 people.
Week 2	Write list of foods to make, check recipe for dessert. Make out shopping list and buy food needed. Try out dessert recipe on the family on Friday night.	Plan ahead. Borrowed mother's easy recipe book, family loved the dessert.	Table will be too small.
Week 3	Make dessert on Saturday. Ask Abdul to do the potatoes and carrots on Sunday morning.	Shabia, my daughter, wants to help make dessert.	Seraj has a fever and had to go to the doctor's.
Week 3 Sunday a.m.	Make plan for the meal. Lay the table!!! Make Lamb Pasanda at 9 a.m. and put in slow oven.		

| Week 3 Sunday afternoon | Serve meal. Abdul helped lay table. | My mother, my worst critic, liked the lamb and dessert. | I forgot to plan washing up help as I was tired and Abdul wanted to play outside. |

MY GOAL LADDER

My goal is

Time:

Week number	Activities to help me achieve my goal	Things that help my progress	Things that block my progress

Choose one of your goals and see if, following Steve's or Razia's example, you can complete your own ladder.

There is a spare Goal Ladder sheet at the back of the book (see p. 294).

Achieving your goals

Here are some tips for success in achieving your goals:

- Try to work on two or three goals at any one time.
- Talk to others; get their views on what goals to focus on at present.
- Consider all the skills and key pieces of information you need to help you reach each goal.
- Plan and carry out one step at a time – each step counts as an achievement. Use the goal ladder sheet.
- Consider what reward you might give yourself when each goal is achieved (see Chapter 7). Write the rewards in your notebook.
- Reward your successes and save the biggest reward until last.

What will happen if you come up against difficulties or barriers? Forewarned is forearmed. It will help if you consider, in advance, how you're going to cope if things don't quite go according to plan. Consider the following questions and jot down the answers in your notebook:

- Are there any barriers that might prevent you from reaching your goal?
- Is there anything that you can do about them at the moment?

In addition, you should record your achievements, either daily or on a weekly basis, as evidence of progress. This will help to reassure you at times when the pain is severe, and you might otherwise be tempted to give up. It's also important not to attempt more than one step of the ladder at any time, or you could fall off! If you do fall off, check what might have caused the setback.

You can use these answers to help reduce the chances of falling off the ladder or having another setback.

And what happens after you have achieved all the goals on your ladder?

Then you can ask yourself the following questions:

- Do you want to continue and build on the same goals?
- Do you want to maintain the same goals?
- Do you want to change to other goals?

Planning and working towards goals is ongoing activity. It can help you make steady progress towards fulfilling your long-term goals.

CHAPTER SUMMARY

- Goal setting is a valuable skill.
- You can use goal setting to help you work towards improving different areas of your life, despite the pain.
- Goal setting can be an enjoyable, rewarding experience, which requires realistic step-by-step planning.
- It may mean using your problem-solving skills to cope with difficulties that occur along the way.
- Rewarding successes or progress in small steps can help keep motivation going and build self-confidence.

7

Giving yourself rewards

This chapter aims to help you understand:

- What rewards are
- How rewards can help change things
- How to reward yourself
- How to create 'Fun prescriptions'

What are rewards?

Having an ice-cream can be a reward; so can a pay packet at the end of the week; a game of cards with a friend; a clean kitchen floor or a 'well done' note to yourself! These are all 'rewards' if they give you a sense of pleasure or achievement.

Rewards are pleasurable activities or things that are fun. They give a sense of pleasure, satisfaction or achievement and help build confidence. Rewards give us the drive to carry out a particular behavior, or support to learn a new one. They encourage 'it's worth a try' thinking. They help us to repeat activities, especially when learning new skills.

We tend to do more of something if we feel rewarded for it, either by ourselves or by others. However, rewards vary according to the individual. Something that is a reward for one person may not be seen as a reward by another.

People tend to avoid situations they expect to be unpleasant. For example, being told off, being shouted at, getting fined, being ignored or rejected are all things we tend to avoid. They are not rewarding. We will do a particular activity less if we are punished for it, or if we lose something as a result.

HOW CAN REWARDS HELP CHANGE THINGS?

Working at change isn't easy. Most people who try to lose weight or give up smoking will agree! This also applies if you have chronic pain. You may very much want to do things differently, but that doesn't always mean that it's easy to change. Using rewards can help change things for the better.

Some people may feel that they do not deserve rewards, especially when they are feeling low, or find themselves unable to work or look after the house. However if you are in pain, rewarding your progress is really vital. It can help you do essential tasks, like washing-up. Rewards can help you make changes that will improve your quality of life.

Try not to compare your progress with what you used to be able to do. Accept the situation and focus on improving things as they are now (see Chapter 15).

HOW TO REWARD YOURSELF

Some people with chronic pain have a lot of demands placed on them, such as looking after children or an elderly relative or working full-time (see Chapter 13). Just coping with everyday activities can be really difficult and rewards can help you cope with these demands.

Here are some ways of working out what is rewarding to you:

1 Think of:

- Things you have or do now
- Things you used to do
- Things you might like to try

Write them down in your notebook.

2 What motivates you, or what used to motivate you? For example, holidays, cinema trips.
3 What gives (or would give) you a sense of pleasure? For example, social rewards (e.g. spending time with people you like to be with).
4 What gives (or would give) you a sense of achievement or satisfaction? For example, activities such as reading a thriller, growing your own roses, watching a video which makes you laugh, seeing a beautiful sunset.

Start by making a list of as many rewards as you can think of now in your notebook. Remember to include small things as well as ambitious and unlikely ones!

Maria had felt for a long time that she did not deserve to reward herself. She was unable to do many things she used to do in the house. She particularly missed looking after her two young grandchildren. So she made a rewards list. She put 'smileys' by the rewards and by her achievements.

Write down your own rewards and achievements in your notebook in two columns. Mark the ones you actually do or have at the moment with tick or smiley face. Remember to think about material things, social activities and things you can do on your own.

MARIA'S REWARDS AND ACHIEVEMENT LIST	
Pleasurable rewards	Sense of achievement
Loved having the grandkids for the weekend. Used to go to craft class years ago. Going on holiday to Spain. Looking at photo albums. Going dancing. A nice cup of tea. A bar of dark chocolate. Wonder in the garden. Long, hot bath with nice bath oil in it. Lunch with my daughter.	Baking for family. Finishing the ironing. Having the best display of roses in the garden. Taking pride in doing a good job at work. Paying for our holiday out of my wages. Passing the beginners' computer course.

Then ask yourself: which rewards could you have now? (These are things you could do or have, with the life situation you are in now, but don't.) For example, **Jim** could have a cafe lunch with his son, but he hadn't thought of it up to now.

Now you can start to make a list of rewarding things that you know that you would like to work towards in the longer term.

Jim decided to choose some rewards he could give himself for working on his goals.

- Having his grandchildren round for a few hours would be a real reward in itself.
- Watching the local rugby match on Saturday if he followed his pacing plan for the garden tasks.
- If he stuck to his breathing relaxation programme each day, he would have a nice cup of tea afterwards with Ann and a hug!

- If he kept to his pacing and relaxation skills for a whole week, he would take Ann to the garden centre and choose some new spring flowering plants and a new hedge trimmer.

Write your own reward plan in your notebook.

Creating a 'fun presciption'

Giving yourself rewards is a vital part of your treatment programme. Now you have had a chance to think about what you find rewarding, look at the ideas for a 'fun prescription' on the next page.

Research has shown that having fun and laughter seems to release the body's 'natural opiates', or endorphins. This may help to reduce pain and increase your sense of well-being. At the very least, it can be a distraction!

Some people with chronic pain feel their sense of humour has kept them going. Some feel they have lost their sense of humour altogether. Planning enjoyable experiences can help you to find it and/or keep it!

A fun prescription helps you to remember to have some fun, even when it is not the first thing that comes to mind. Being in pain can make it harder to enjoy yourself; you can get out of practice at taking pleasure in things.

As you practise having more fun and gradually increase what you can do, it will get easier. This is why it is important to plan something rewarding every day.

Here is an example of a fun prescription:

FUN PRESCRIPTION

Name: Jim
Date: 11/6/04

50 mg of fun three times a day (at least)
For maximum benefit, use imagination!

- Watch a funny video.
- Watch a championship football match on TV.
- Try out a new supper recipe.
- Get a bird feeder for the garden.
- Start a scrapbook of silly cartoons.
- Phone someone I enjoy talking to.
- Invite a friend round to play cards.
- Design a silly T-shirt.
- Go somewhere new.
- Listen to that tango music.
- Juggle the lemons from the fruit bowl!

Do not discontinue this treatment without medical advice!

Now write your own fun prescription in your notebook! Remember to add to it as more ideas occur to you. Try to include smaller rewards for everyday, and some larger ones to reward yourself for persistence, or for reaching a longer-term target you have set yourself.

CHAPTER SUMMARY

- Rewards are a vital part of managing chronic pain. They can help you to keep going when 'the going gets tough'.
- Rewards help you appreciate your own efforts and build self-confidence while you are working to achieve your goals.
- Rewards can include material things like gifts; social rewards, such as having someone smile at you; or other activities that give a sense of pleasure or achievement.
- It is important to find rewards that work for you, not necessarily what others find rewarding.

- Sometimes it can feel as if you don't 'deserve' a reward, but they are an important part of achieving your goals.
- They can help you to rediscover pleasure and fun, and a 'fun prescription' gives you an opportunity to remember to enjoy yourself every day.

8

Understanding pacing skills

This chapter aims to help you to understand:

- What pacing is
- What the different styles of pacing are
- How to change your pacing style
- How to deal with barriers to realistic pacing

What is pacing?

Pacing is a valuable self-help skill for managing chronic pain. It enables you to plan and monitor your activities so that you are more in control of your everyday life and the pain.

Finding a helpful pacing style means:

- Reaching a balanced pattern of varied activity at a steady pace, using time or distance not pain as a guide.
- Doing some activity even at times when you don't feel like it – for instance, when you are tired, in pain or feeling down.
- Doing the same or similar levels of activity every day.
- Not overdoing activities on better days.

- Not under-doing activities on difficult days, despite pain, low mood or other problems.
- Steadily increasing the amount you do and the types of activity over time.

To many people with chronic pain, it seems sensible to make plans and do activities based on the amount of pain experienced at the time. This can be helpful for acute pain after an injury. However, if it continues for more than a month or two, it may mean that the pain is in control of you and not the other way around! This is because your level of activity is set by the amount of pain (see Chapter 2 and Chapter 6).

In the long term, this way of pacing may mean that you achieve less, lose confidence, become tired more easily, lose physical fitness, become irritable or bad-tempered, lose contact with family, friends and work colleagues, have more pain, lack energy and drive, and lose motivation.

Pacing is an important skill to master, as it can help you:

- Do more, over time, by yourself or with family and friends
- Have more control over the pain
- Have fewer setbacks
- Help you use less medicines and have fewer side-effects

Learning to pace better takes practice, especially if you are new to the idea. It is just like learning to ride a bike, use a new cooker or do a watercolour painting. We all make mistakes at first. People with chronic pain who have learnt the skill of pacing have found it is well worth the time and effort. They report feeling better and more confident about themselves.

Let's take **Jim** as an example. To help him pace better, Jim planned some time for relaxed breathing and did some stretches. He also planned his activities more carefully. He was delighted as he was able to do more around the garden and felt less tired. He asked his wife, Ann, to help him to pace better. She called him to collect a drink or a piece of fruit every 30 minutes to take to the garden. This meant he had a regular break from his task.

What are the different styles of pacing?

Generally there are two styles of pacing that are unhelpful for people with chronic pain, overactive and underactive. They both have advantages and disadvantages.

Look at the information below and decide which pacing style you currently use. It may be a mixture of both.

OVERACTIVE PACING

This means doing too **much** activity or too many tasks over a short space of time. This may happen if you are having a good day, with less pain, or your mood is better.

UNDERACTIVE PACING

This means that you are doing too **little** activity to help keep strength, stamina and flexibility in your muscles, ligaments, joints and bones. More of your time is spent resting, sitting or lying down. This is understandable, especially if there is a lot of pain. However, it may in itself add to your pain, as lack of fitness makes muscles and other tissues tight and weak. They then tire more easily when used or stretched (see Chapter 9), leading to more pain.

What type of pacing style do you use at present?

You can identify your pacing style by using the lists below. Tick those behaviors or actions you use at present. If you are having problems identifying your current pacing style using the lists, ask a friend, partner or family member to help you. They will often be more aware of your pattern of activity and unhelpful pacing styles.

LIST A

If pain levels are low, do you:

1 Try to make up for all the things you haven't done or achieved because the pain stopped you?
2 Fit in as much as possible until the pain level is very high?
3 Do activities as fast as possible until the pain level is very high?
4 Do very little so as to keep the pain level low?
5 Focus on doing important activities at a steady pace with regular breaks?

LIST B

If pain levels are high, do you:

1 Keep going with all your activities, despite the pain, with few or no breaks?
2 Put a brave face on it and keep 'battling on' with activities?
3 Reduce all your activity until pain gets lower?
4 Reduce high standards for activities for the high pain period?
5 Plan activities that are realistic?

6 Decide on important activities?

7 Focus on doing important activities at a steady pace, with regular breaks?

If you ticked the first three items in list A or or the first two items in list B, then you are using an overactive style. If you ticked number 4 in list A or number 3 in list B, then you may be using an underactive type of pacing. Alternatively, you may have ticked a mix of both pacing styles, which is quite common.

If you are finding this task hard, read about Jim's and Razia's daily routines over the next few pages. This may help you work out your current pacing style.

LIST C

Helpful pacing style

Below are the features of a helpful pacing style:

- Focus on doing important activities at a steady pace with regular breaks.
- Reduce high standards for activities for the high pain period.
- Plan activities that are realistic.
- Decide on important activities.

These are ways of pacing activities that will put you in control and help you manage the pain.

Consider these two examples of pacing styles.

Jim

Jim is 59 years old. He is married to Ann who has a heart problem. Jim retired as a teacher two years ago, because of his chest and abdomen pain. Since his retirement, he has taken on many household tasks to fill his day and to help Ann because of her heart problems. He shops every day, prepares and cooks all the meals. He does all the washing and ironing. He has a large garden and spends the rest of his time weeding, planting out and mowing the lawn. He thinks he must get these jobs done so that Ann won't feel worried or stressed. He used to enjoy walking and reading but he has difficulty finding time. He is becoming exhausted and has noticed, to his surprise, that his pain is worse.

Jim's pacing style can be described as overactive. It has advantages and disadvantages.

TABLE 8.1: JIM'S PACING STYLE

Advantages	Disadvantages
Things 'get done' around the house and garden, as Jim is able to meet the needs of his wife, Ann, and his family. He feels useful. He is glad Ann has less to do and is under less stress.	Jim is becoming less useful and tired, as he cannot finish jobs. He is increasing his pain and may even trigger a setback. Jim is becoming irritable and withdrawn. Ann may worry about Jim doing too much and his pain increasing.

What would you suggest to help Jim pace better? Use your notebook and write four ways he could improve his pacing?

Razia

Razia finds the pain from her fibromyalgia unpredictable and often rests when she has bad pain days. She wanted to stay active because of the children. She saw the physiotherapist and was given stretch exercises to help her become more active. The stretches made her body hurt more, so she did not keep her next appointment. The doctor has told Razia that physiotherapy can't help her if she doesn't go to the appointments. Razia finds that if she does very few activities then her pain eases up. She has stopped all housework and sleeps a lot. Her parents are doing all the shopping and childcare, especially after school. She thinks she should meet all her children's needs herself. She believes the pain is making her tired and irritable, and spoiling daily life. Razia has lost confidence and sees herself as a 'useless mother'.

Razia's pacing style can be described as underactive. It has advantages and disadvantages.

TABLE 8.2: RAZIA'S PACING STYLE	
Advantages	Disadvantages
In the short term, Razia may experience less pain, and may get a few essential things done at home.	Razia's pain is worse and lasts longer because of the effects of inactivity on her body, e.g. stiff joints and weak muscles. She feels tired so she sleeps during the day. Loss of fitness. Irritable and cross with the children. Loss of confidence to do things. Less time and enjoyment with her children and family.

What would you suggest to help Razia pace better? Using your notebook and write four ways she could improve her pacing?

- What are the advantages and disadvantages of your own pacing style?
- Would you say your style is overactive, underactive, a mixture of overactive and underactive, or sensible (as in List C on page 121)?

How to change your pacing style

List the advantages and disadvantages of your pacing style, in two columns, in your notebook.

Then ask yourself:

- Do the advantages outweigh the disadvantages?
- Do I need to change my pacing style?
- Why change an unhelpful pacing style?

Many people feel worried about changing their style of pacing, especially if they believe that they are 'managing' their pain. However people with chronic pain report that changing their style of pacing has many benefits, such as:

- More energy and 'get up and go'
- Better sleep patterns
- Stronger muscles
- Greater flexibility
- Doing and achieving more
- Better social life
- Brighter moods, more enjoyment, fun and more confidence
- Less pain
- Reduced number and length of setbacks

List the advantages and disadvantages of changing your pacing style, in two columns, in your notebook.

You may not feel ready to change your pacing style at present. However, it may help to keep revisiting this chapter. Developing a sensible, balanced pacing style is one of the best ways to manage chronic pain.

Experimenting

It may help to experiment with making small changes in your pacing style. This will enable you to test out whether your beliefs are accurate. Sometimes you might believe that a task or activity should be done and completed at a particular time. This may be based on evidence – e.g. that if it is a better day then you must get it done now or else it could be many days before you get another chance. You might then keep going with the activity or task with no breaks, despite a high or increasing level of pain. The job will be completed but you may be disabled by the pain and end up feeling distressed. Instead, try experimenting with an alternative thought, like 'If I plan in some breaks, does the job take longer and is the pain level worse?' or 'If I plan and spread the job over two days, then do I still achieve the job and is the pain worse?' By experimenting, many people discover that the job takes a little longer. They also find they are in less pain and feel less tired, have less distress and still achieve their goal. They realize they have much more control over their pain than they thought they did.

Planning

First be clear about what you would like to change. Here are some suggestions:

- Make a plan for each day or week and try to stick to it, where possible.
- Put your activities in order of importance. Then choose the top two or three – those that *must* be done in that day or week.
- Try not to push yourself on a good day and risk a setback.
- Make sure you do some activity even on a bad day.
- Tell other people what you are doing and why.
- Inform others of how they can help.
- Identify any barriers to changing your pacing style.
- Think about how you and others can tackle those barriers.
- Build in strategies that may help you to achieve your aim e.g. a five-minute rest, relaxed breathing or a couple of stretches (see Chapter 9).
- Build in rewards for helpful changes (see Chapter 7) and don't forget to give yourself a 'pat on the back'.

Now write down what you want to change in your own pacing style. For instance, Jim wanted to change his overactive style of pacing. He started by giving himself more breaks in the morning. He asked Ann to help him. They agreed that she would call him for a drink or fruit snack every 30 minutes.

Priorities

Choose the most important things to work on first. You might include:

- Leisure activities and hobbies, e.g. swimming, walking, planting in the garden, making cards.
- Social activities, e.g. going to see a film at the cinema.
- Household tasks, e.g. ironing clothes.
- Self-care, e.g. styling your hair, cooking a healthy meal.
- Work (paid or voluntary), e.g. in a local charity shop.

There are different ways to change your pacing style. Here are some suggestions.

STEP ONE

List each activity and record the time it took you on a recent **good** day and a recent **bad** day (see Razia's Pacing Plan below).

STEP TWO

Under the 'Everyday plan' heading, write the number of minutes in which you could **realistically** carry out that activity every day, despite pain.

STEP THREE

Under the 'Times per day' heading, write down the number of times you could repeat the activity. It may help to break tasks down into smaller activities: e.g. ironing for 10-minute periods; or painting a wall, then having a rest break (see Razia's Daily Activity Plan below).

Here is Razia's Pacing Plan, as an example:

TABLE 8.3: RAZIA'S PACING PLAN

Activity	Good day	Bad day	Everyday plan	Times per day
Standing and cooking	20 mins	10 mins	12 mins	6
Lying down for rest	15 mins	65 mins	25 mins	2
Walking	20 mins	8 mins	14 mins	2

This means that Razia plans to stand and cook for 12 minutes, six times per day. After each 12-minute cooking session, she will take a 5-minute break to sit down. Then, Razia could walk around and do three specific stretches for 4 minutes. See chapter 9. She could then return to standing to cook or move on to another activity.

Razia then gradually increases the everyday plan time by 2 or 3 minutes every four or five days. For example, after a month she has increased in her everyday plan her standing activities, like cooking, to 22 minutes. She rewards herself with her favourite fruit in season, mangoes. She starts thinking about other things she could do with the children.

Now try filling in your own Pacing Plan on the opposite page. Pacing means thinking about:

- How often to do an activity.
- How long to spend sensibly at an activity.
- When to do it in a typical day.

It sometimes means reducing unhelpful activities and increasing others. For example, Razia realized her underactive pacing style meant she needed to reduce her long periods of rest in bed. She still had breaks but planned fewer and shorter rest times (see her Pacing Plan above). This helped her fitness increase steadily.

TABLE 8.4: YOUR PACING PLAN				
Activity	Good day	Bad day	Everyday plan	Times per day
Sitting				
Standing				
Lying				
Walking				
Other e.g.: work				
hobbies				
driving				
relaxation				
Own activity e.g., exercises				

Razia's Daily Activity Plan (see overleaf) shows how she **planned** parts of her days, putting in her **priorities**, like taking the children to school. Her plan helped her **pace**. At the end of the day she could see she was more active (especially with the children), getting fitter and still had some rest times. She shared her plan with Hassian, her husband, and he was very supportive and offered some ideas too.

RAZIA'S DAILY ACTIVITY PLAN

Time period	Activity
7.00 a.m.	Get up. Do some stretching. *Rest*.
7.30 a.m.	Shower and make a drink. *Rest*.
8.30 a.m.	Walk the children to school. *Rest*.
9.15 a.m.	Make breakfast. *Rest* 25 minutes.
10.30 a.m.	Go to the shops for 30 minutes.
12.30 p.m.	Make lunch. *Rest*.
2.00 p.m.	Do stretches and relaxation.
3.00 p.m.	Tidy living room. Visit mother. *Rest*.
4.00 p.m.	Exercise – 20 minutes; 10 minutes walk up street and 10 minutes back home.
5.00 p.m.	Prepare evening meal. *Rest*. Cook meal.
6.00 p.m.	Meal, and watch TV with family.
7.00 p.m.	Help children with reading and getting ready for bed by 8.00 p.m.
8.30 p.m.	Talk to Hassian about family wedding.
10.00 p.m.	Bed at 10.15 p.m.; use deep-breathing relaxation. If wake, get up and try three stretches or relaxation; maybe read for ten minutes. No TV.

Here is a Daily Activity Plan for your own use. There is a spare Daily Activity Plan sheet, if you need it, at the back of the book (see p. 295).

DAILY ACTIVITY PLAN

Time period	Activity
7.00 a.m.	
7.30 a.m.	
8.30 a.m.	
9.30 a.m.	
10.30 a.m.	
11.30 a.m.	
12.30 p.m.	
2.00 p.m.	
3.00 p.m.	
4.00 p.m.	
5.00 p.m.	
6.00 p.m.	
7.00 p.m.	
8.00 p.m.	
9.00 p.m.	
10.00 p.m.	
11.00 p.m.	
12.00 a.m.–7.00 a.m.	

How to deal with barriers to realistic pacing

Start by trying to work out what sort of situations might stop you from pacing more effectively. For instance:

- Having to meet a deadline at work
- Being ill, e.g. having flu
- Having to cope with family demands
- Having to deal with an emergency
- Having a good or bad pain day

In your notebook, write down any barriers that you are facing at the moment.

Then, next to each barrier, write down what you can do to tackle it (see Chapters 6, 7, 9, 10 and 16 for ideas).

Here are some tips for success in changing your pacing style:

- Time yourself while doing each activity.
- Don't say 'I'll just do 5 more minutes' or 'I'll just finish this bit'. This type of thinking leads to overactive pacing.
- Try and do some activity on bad days, even if it's only 5 minutes. Be aware of unhelpful negative thinking or fearful predictions on difficult pain days. This type of thinking can reduce your activity further, so experiment.
- Steadily increase the level of your activity. For example, you could gradually lengthen the time you spend driving the car from 10 minutes to 20 minutes over a three-week period.
- Record and reward your achievements.

CHAPTER SUMMARY

- Pacing is an important skill that can improve all aspects of your life. Identifying your pacing style and making changes helps you balance activities and breaks.
- If you are underactive, you need to steadily pace yourself towards a more active life. If you are overactive, you need to plan more rest times and relaxation.
- If you have a mixed pacing style, you need to monitor your activity. Get to know the situations, times or thinking that trigger a period of overactivity or underactivity.
- Plan each day and choose what is important to achieve. Priorities are a vital part of pacing skills. Experiment with your Daily Activity Plan, especially with finding a balance between activities and rest or relaxation breaks. Reward yourself often, especially for effort.

9

Getting fitter and being more active

This chapter aims to help you understand:

- How being more active can help you manage your pain
- How to assess your present activity level
- Frequently asked questions about increasing physical activity
- How to get started on a basic exercise programme

TIP

Don't be tempted to skip this section. However, just reading it won't make you fitter or more active. Action is called for, and changes to your daily routine may need to be made!

How being more active can help you manage your pain

People with chronic pain say that regular daily physical activity is **vital** to manage the impact of pain on their lives. Being active has so many benefits that help to make a real difference to you and the quality of your life. Physical activity may simply mean doing an activity faster, more often or for longer – for example, getting off the bus one stop earlier, stretching to put the plates on a higher shelf, or using the stairs more.

Initially many people with pain are told to rest as part of their treatment. Rest is helpful in the early days of an injury or setback, to reduce pain and help with healing. But doctors and physiotherapists now realize that rest is only beneficial for a short time – one to three days. Being inactive for longer does not help to rebuild fitness and so adds to the problems.

Sometimes people with pain are unsure when it is safe to move, exercise and return to normal physical activities, such as walking to the shop for a newspaper or doing the ironing. Common sense might suggest that we should judge our level of recovery by the amount of pain we feel. However this approach is not helpful, as hurt is not the same as harm in chronic pain. (For more on this, see Chapter 2.)

Increasing activity with chronic pain may be difficult. The pain can feel as bad as when it started, months or even years ago. Understandably, people with chronic pain often think they should not increase activity if they still have pain. However, gradually increasing your activity level, at a steady pace, can prove very successful and rewarding.

Trying to get fitter: What does having more pain mean?

Starting to increase activities and exercises can mean experiencing new or different aches and pains at first. These aches and pains might make you think:

- *This exercise has made me worse.*
- *This new ache means that I have injured myself again and I am back to square one.*
- *This activity is bad for me. I should stop and not do it again.*

Actually, new aches and pains can be normal. They may not be connected to your main area of chronic pain. For example, you would have aches and pains if you had:

- Not dug the garden for a year, then dug it over on the first day of spring.
- Not washed the car for six months, then given it a full clean, including the inside.
- Decorated the bedroom – painting, scraping and hanging wallpaper for the first time in five years.

You can probably think of other examples from your own experience. Use your notebook to write them down.

Why do these types of activity cause aches and pains?

The feeling of aching and stiffness after activity is because muscles, ligaments, tendons, joints and scar tissues have become stiff, tight and less flexible over time. There are many reasons for pain following an increase in physical activity. You may have:

- Done too much
- Done it too quickly
- Be less fit than you used to be
- Be unused to doing this type of activity

TIP

Pain is not always a sign that we have damaged or injured ourselves. (See Chapter 2.)

As your body gets used to being more active, the aches and pains will often gradually reduce and settle (see Chapter 8).

Assessing your present activity level

Are you more or less active than you were a year ago?

If **less** active, how has your life changed? Write down any changes you have noticed in your notebook.

If **more** active, again write down any changes you have noticed.

Becoming less active can happen suddenly or slowly over time. Have you cut down on or stopped doing any activities because of your pain problem? If so, write them down in your notebook.

You may have noticed some advantages in reducing activity levels. Tick any that fit your own situation:

❑ Not having to take as many painkillers
❑ Having less pain
❑ Not having to do jobs or activities like vacuuming or making the beds

❑ Not having setbacks with pain
❑ Sleeping better most nights
❑ Moods remaining stable
❑ Others?

People in pain may find that they stop doing some activities or getting into certain positions – for example, bending to take food out of the oven. Sometimes this is done to reduce the amount of pain. At other times there is a fear of making the pain worse or even getting stuck in one position!

It is important to understand that moving more freely and loosely is more likely to get you back to your usual activities. Your body is designed to allow movement in lots of different directions. Moving will help your body cope with pain better.

TIP

Remember, the longer you continue to rest, the harder it becomes to get going again.

There may also be some disadvantages in reducing your activity level. Tick any that fit your own situation:

❑ More joint and muscle stiffness
❑ Loss of movement
❑ Loss of stamina
❑ Poor sleep
❑ Feeling tired
❑ Shortening of scar tissue
❑ Loss of muscle strength

❑ Mood changes, e.g. feeling down, low, frustrated or angry, as cannot do things
❑ Higher risk of osteoporosis
❑ Higher risk of developing heart disease
❑ Fewer endorphins to reduce pain and lift moods
❑ Returning to normal activities becomes more difficult
❑ Poor circulation of blood, especially in the arms and legs
❑ Poor sex life
❑ Others?

There are many myths about physical activity and exercise. How many of these have you heard before?

- It has to hurt to do you any good.
- No pain, no gain.
- You need to go to a gym to get proper exercise.
- You have to do a lot of it before you feel any benefit.
- Exercise makes you tired.
- You need special clothes.
- Exercise damages joints.
- Exercise will make your pain worse.
- Others?

Frequently asked questions about increasing physical activity

'WHAT DOES BEING PHYSICALLY ACTIVE MEAN?'

There are three components to being physically active:

Stamina: Being able to 'keep going' at jobs, hobbies and exercises.

Flexibility: Being able to use a wide range of movements, e.g. to reach down to put your socks on or reach into your back pocket.

Strength: Being able to do hard work, like digging, lifting or vacuuming.

'WHAT IS FITNESS?'

Fitness means having the physical and mental ability to carry out the daily activities needed for work or leisure.

Increasing physical activity may mean following a planned exercise routine.

Consider which of the three parts of becoming fit and active you would like to work on. Do you want more strength, more stamina or more flexibility? You may even want all three!

'HOW WILL I FEEL WHEN I START INCREASING MY ACTIVITY LEVEL?'

You may feel more tired at first, and you may develop new aches and pains. This is normal and will get easier with time. Initially, you may only be able to manage quite a limited amount of physical activity because of poor stamina and strength. Getting started and continuing every day can be a real effort, so remember to reward yourself (see Chapter 7).

'WHEN SHOULD I EXPECT TO FEEL A CHANGE AS A RESULT OF INCREASING MY ACTIVITY?'

A change is usually felt within a few days and real improvement would be felt at three to four weeks. These changes get more noticeable, depending on what activity you choose, how often you do it and how long you keep it going. Slowly your fitness will increase.

'HOW WILL PHYSICAL ACTIVITY HELP ME MANAGE PAIN, ESPECIALLY IF IT MAKES ME ACHE?'

It will:

- Help you to do and achieve more every day
- Lift your mood
- Help you get back to work and hobbies
- Improve your muscle bulk and strength
- Reduce your joint stiffness
- Improve your flexibility
- Stretch scar tissue
- Control your weight and improve your body shape
- Improve your stamina
- Improve your sex life
- Improve your sleep pattern
- Increase your bone strength
- Reduce your blood pressure and risk of heart disease
- Release your body's natural painkillers, endorphins
- Help you get through setbacks
- Help you feel good about yourself
- Help you gain more confidence to get on with your life

'I'VE NEVER BEEN VERY ACTIVE SO WHAT CAN I DO?'

Increasing your activity levels and committing to getting fitter doesn't have to mean running around a football pitch or playing tennis. Getting fitter can start at any age and from any level of fitness. There are many ways of increasing your activity levels to improve stamina, flexibility and strength, such as:

- Using the stairs more often
- Hanging out the washing
- Standing up to do the ironing or cooking
- Cycling inside on a static bike or outside
- Parking the car and walking further to the shops
- Walking at a faster pace
- Taking a shower and stretching more
- Doing exercises at home on a mat
- Stretching to wash the windows
- Dusting a room
- Dancing to a favourite song
- Getting off the bus two stops earlier and walking home
- Playing hide and seek with the grandchildren

Apart from improving your fitness, there are a lot of other advantages to getting more active. For instance, you can get out more, meet new people, reduce your stress levels, take your mind off your worries, and lose some weight.

'HOW DO I START GETTING FITTER?'

Imagine that your best friend is about to start a fitness programme. She has a pain problem. What type of programme would you suggest to her? Perhaps you would say:

- Pace and plan it – little and often (see Chapter 8).
- Set yourself short-term and long-term goals (see Chapter 6).
- Use a timer – and stick to it. No extra minutes!

- Record the number of exercises on a sheet or in a diary. Look back at it regularly to see your progress.
- In the beginning it helps to choose a set time each day.
- Don't push yourself too far, too fast.
- Gradually increase the amount you do over several weeks.
- Stick at it but remember that changes take time!
- Get someone else involved.
- Find activities that you enjoy.
- Don't push through the pain.
- Take adequate pain relief beforehand.
- Reward yourself (see Chapter 7).
- Put on some music or a video.
- When the 'feel good factor' kicks in, don't do more repetitions of an exercise or a few extra minutes.
- Vary the types of physical activity.
- Build in some exercises or activities to improve stamina, flexibility and strength daily. Simply get out of breath more often!
- Think of the advantages of becoming more active.

What physical activity goals would you like to achieve? For instance, perhaps you want to be able to walk to the local shop? Use your goal sheet or your notebook. Then work out your physical activity plan.

You will probably need some strategies to keep you going and enable you to check your achievements. Here are some ideas. Tick those that you think you could use:

❑ Use a diary of activity goals. Include time to be spent on each activity and reward when you achieve it.
❑ Change your routine often, and remember to begin again slowly.

❑ Reward yourself often.
❑ Recognize and acknowledge your improvements.
❑ Accept praise and compliments.
❑ Work with a friend.
❑ Work on strength one day and stamina or flexibility the next.

'WHAT ABOUT SETBACKS?'

Tick those that may cause an activity setback for you?

❑ Poor weather
❑ A pain increase
❑ Holiday
❑ Family crisis
❑ Work
❑ Childcare arrangements
❑ Fatigue
❑ Others?

Setbacks happen but it is important to understand why they happen, and see what we can learn from them (see Chapter 16).

How to get started on a basic exercise programme

Here are some suggestions for a basic exercise programme that will begin to improve your strength and flexibility. Your stamina will improve with any activity that makes your heart beat faster and stronger, e.g. climbing stairs, walking uphill, washing the car, or sweeping the yard. It helps your heart become fitter if it beats faster and you become slightly breathless.

Note: Before thinking about doing these exercises, make sure you read all the sections above.

You will need:

- A chair
- Floor space and a mat or blanket
- Loose, comfortable clothing
- Some time!

HOW DO YOU 'WARM UP' AND 'COOL DOWN'?

A 'warm up' means using gentle, relatively slow movements to prepare your body for exercise – for example, walking for 5 minutes, going up and down the stairs a couple of times, or anything that makes you breathe a little faster and gives you a warm feeling.

A 'cool down' means using gentle movements or stretches to help the body recover from exercise. An example of a 'cool down' may be walking on the spot and letting your arms swing by your sides for 3–5 minutes.

All the exercises overleaf marked with an (S) can be used as stretches.

TIP

Remember that, initially, the warm up may be enough.

Illustrations of the following exercises can be found in the Appendix pages 298–304.

Strength exercises – do slowly

NECK

Starting position: Sit down, face forwards

1 Bring your chin down towards your chest and then up towards the ceiling. (S)
2 Look over to your left shoulder, return to facing forwards, then look over to your right shoulder. (S)
3 Bring your ear down towards the shoulder on the left, and then do the same to the right side. (S)

SHOULDERS AND ARMS

Starting position: Sit or stand, arms down by your sides

4 Bring your shoulders up towards your ears. (S)
5 Push your shoulders down towards the floor. (S)
6 Bring your shoulders forwards to meet each other at the front of your body. (S)
7 Pull your shoulders backwards to meet each other at the back of your body. (S)
8 Lift your arms forwards and up above your head. (S)
9 Lift your arms sideways and up above your head. (S)
10 Place your hands on top of your head and slide them down the back of your head towards the floor. (S)
11 Place your hands on your bottom and slide them up towards your head. (S)
12 With arms down by your side, bring your hands up to touch the front of your shoulders. You may add a small weight, like a can of beans in each hand for any of the arm exercises.

LOWER BACK

Starting position A: Sitting on a chair with legs straight out

13 Let your hands slide down the front of your legs towards your feet.
14 Let your back slouch into a C shape and then sit upright again.

Starting position B: Lying on your back with your knees bent up and feet flat on the floor or bed

15 Keeping your knees together, let them roll from side to side. Keep your shoulders flat on the floor. (S)
16 Place your hands on the front of your thighs and let them slide up towards the tops of your knees, keeping your chin tucked in.

HIPS

Starting position: Standing up and facing forwards

17 Take 3 steps to the left and then 3 steps to the right.
18 Take 3 steps backwards, then 3 steps forwards.
19 Face up a flight of stairs or a step. Step up onto the loweststep, then bring the other foot up onto the same step.

KNEES

Starting position: Sitting in a chair

20 Straighten one leg out, then return and straighten the other. (S)
21 Stand up from a sitting position, trying not to use your hands to help. The lower the chair, the harder it is!

ANKLE

Starting position: Standing up, facing a windowsill or a kitchen work surface

22 Push downwards through your hands into the surface and move up on to tip toes, as if looking over a high fence.

Note: Everybody can become more physically active. However, it may be sensible to inform your doctor that you plan to do more activity. You must tell your doctor that you plan to do more exercise or activity if you have any heart condition, such as severe angina or a previous heart attack, or diabetes, or dizziness or blurred vision when you turn your head.

Stretches for flexibility

Regular stretches will improve your flexibility so that, for instance, you will be able to get dressed, brush your hair and tie your shoelaces more easily. You could do some stretches as part of your cool-down routine. Choose two or three of them.

To get full benefit from the stretches, you need to:

- Perform one of the above exercises marked with an (S). When your tissues feel tight, hold still in that position. **Do not bounce or jerk.**
- Hold each stretch for 5 seconds to begin with. Then gradually, over a period of a few weeks, work up to a 15-second hold. Return to the given starting position.
- Stretches only need to be performed once during each exercise session.
- Keep your breathing steady. You should not feel out of breath. If you do, then ease off a little as you are working too hard.

- Stretch on a regular basis. Aim to do **2–3 stretches 3–4 times** per day.

Note: The stretches should not be painful. If there is pain then ease off the stretch a little.

WORKING OUT YOUR OWN EXERCISE PROGRAMME

From the list above, choose five strength exercises that you plan to continue – even on a bad day or during a setback. Write them in your notebook.

From the list above, choose three stretches that you plan to continue – even on a bad day or during a setback. Write them in your notebook.

Remember to add in some walking, swimming, dancing or cycling to improve your stamina.

It may help to work with a physiotherapist or fitness coach or personal trainer.

CHAPTER SUMMARY

- Everybody can improve their physical activity and fitness levels, despite pain.
- Improving your activity levels will help you feel good and reduce the impact of pain on your life.
- New aches and pain are normal when you begin increasing your physical activity.
- Little and often is the key. Build up slowly and regularly over a few weeks.
- Build in a mixture of regular daily activities to improve your stamina, strength and flexibility.
- Vary your activities. Make sure that you enjoy them and reward yourself often.
- For more ideas about activity and fitness levels, see the Useful Information section at the back of this book.

10

Understanding problem-solving

This chapter aims to help you understand more about:

- What problem-solving is
- The main steps in problem-solving
- How to put the problem-solving process into practice

What is problem-solving?

Problem-solving is a skill that can help you to cope with many different life problems. These problems may be caused by chronic pain, or by other circumstances. You can use problem-solving to help find the coping strategies that work best for you.

Problem-solving gives you a step-by-step approach to dealing with difficulties. It enables you to face a problem and come up with a plan to try to deal with it. Problem-solving is also a useful way to plan and achieve your goals. This could be anything from organizing limited household finances to getting an awkward glass jar open. Problem-solving can help you to be more confident about overcoming challenges that you face, especially pain. It can put you more in control and help you manage difficulties. It can help you to work out whether something really can be changed or not.

If it can't be changed, problem-solving can help you deal with the unpleasant emotions or thoughts you may have because you cannot change it.

The main steps in problem-solving

There are five main steps in problem-solving.

STEP 1: RECOGNIZE AND DEFINE THE PROBLEM

This means realizing that something is in fact a problem, and describing it. This can give you time to think. Recognizing that there is a problem also means that you can choose **how** to deal with it. You can decide how important it is to do something about it (or not!). This puts you more in control of your response. It offers an alternative way of dealing with problems – instead of acting on 'first impulse' without considering alternatives, or 'doing nothing' and hoping the problem will go away. Sometimes unpleasant emotions (such as feeling low or worried) can give you clues as to where the problem lies. If you realize that something is making you feel like this, you can then decide how much of a problem it is to you, and choose what to do next.

Defining the problem means being clear about exactly what the problem is. You can try talking it through with someone until you are able to write it down. Or you can make rough notes for yourself until you can write it down clearly.

For example, **Steve** wrote down his problem like this:

'Getting fed-up and frustrated, which happens when I think about being stuck in the house all the time.'

TIP

If it turns out to be a number of different problems, choose one to concentrate on first. Or you can break a large problem down into parts. You may already have some experience of breaking things down into steps from working on your pacing skills in Chapter 8.

STEP 2: LIST ALL POSSIBLE SOLUTIONS

Write down all the ways in which the problem might get solved. List all the ideas you can come up with, even 'bad' or 'silly' suggestions. If nothing comes to mind, think of the most ridiculous ideas possible, and take it from there! You can even think first of what would make the problem worse. At least then you can write down 'doing the opposite'! If you are discussing it with someone else, get the other person to think of ideas, too. See how many ideas you can come up with. At this stage, don't 'filter out' or discuss the advantages of any suggestions. Just jot them down in your notebook.

Steve thought of the following ideas – with help from his friend Malcolm:

- Get my neighbour to take me out
- Go on a romantic weekend to Paris with Nicole
- Join a wine-making club
- Get my brother to let me baby-sit for my nephew
- Move house
- Visit my friend Paul more often
- Go down the pub
- Blow up the house
- Redecorate
- Keep my eyes shut all day

- Try staying in the house more so I get used to it
- Go for a walk to the park
- Sit in the garden

STEP 3: LIST THE ADVANTAGES AND DISADVANTAGES OF EACH POSSIBLE SOLUTION

Now go through your list, and highlight the main advantages and disadvantages of each solution.

What would the consequences be:

- In the short term and in the long term?
- For you, and for others?

Bear in mind the resources that you have now, including time, skills and money.

Steve listed the advantages and disadvantages opposite.

STEP 4: CHOOSE THE 'BEST' SOLUTION

From your list, choose the solution that you are most likely to be able to carry out, given your present circumstances. It may not be the 'perfect' answer, but at least it gives you an option to try. Remember to plan each step, think about any problems or hitches that might arise, and practise the difficult parts beforehand.

Steve decided: The best solution at present is to go and see my friend, Paul, more often.

I will phone up this afternoon and try to arrange a short visit this week.

Possible hitches?

If he's not in, I will either leave a message or try again.

TABLE 10.1: STEVE'S LIST OF ADVANTAGES AND DISADVANTAGES

Advantages	Disadvantages
Get Mick my neighbour to take me out	Could do but he talks about stuff I'm not that bothered about.
Go on a romantic weekend to Paris with Nicole	We cannot afford to with so many bills to pay??
Join a wine-making club	Interesting, but I'm not supposed to drink on these tablets.
Get brother to let me baby-sit	His four walls might be more interesting than mine but I am not up to dealing with a two-year-old jumping on me, wherever it is.
Move house	Yeah, yeah. Lovely idea, but where do I get the money and energy from? And anyway I'd still be stuck in a house, just a different one.
Visit my friend Paul more often	Sounds OK – he always says 'pop round any time'. What if he's busy? Could phone and arrange a good time to go.
Go down the pub, play darts	Who with?? If I arrange it I may have a bad night and then I cannot be bothered.
Blow up the house	Well, I was short of ideas . . .
Redecorate	OK but it wouldn't change the 'being stuck' bit much.
Keep my eyes shut all day	Very funny, Nicole would laugh at me.
Try staying in the house more so I get used to it	I think if I stayed in more, the problem would be where to get the straitjacket!
Go for a walk to the park	I'm working on getting about already – but I want a person to talk to as well.
Sit in the garden	Can do, but see above.

If I have no luck getting hold of him, I will send him a text message after three days and ask him to phone.

If we have fun, we will do it again. If not, I can have another look at my list.

Review in two weeks.

STEP 5: REVIEW YOUR PROGRESS

Decide when you will review your progress in carrying out your plan. Have a look at how you got on with each step. Remember to praise yourself for effort, rather than achievement.

You may need to revise your plans, and set another review as you go along. Keep problem-solving until you have achieved your goal, or resolved the stress. If you still find that something can't be changed, then at least you will know that you have tried. You can use problem-solving to help you to deal with feelings, such as anger or sadness, which may arise. You could also try talking your feelings through, focusing on something else, or finding ways of accepting the way things have turned out (see Chapter 15).

Steve reviewed his progress after two weeks:

I have been round to Paul's house twice, and we are off to the garden centre tomorrow. It's a good start. I want to do other things as well now – I feel a bit better. Maybe I'll try a photography evening class?

Putting the problem-solving process into practise

Here's a problem-solving guide for you to use with your own problems. Write out all the steps in your notebook.

Problem-solving guide

STEP 1: DEFINE THE PROBLEM

What is the problem or goal?

Talk it through, or make notes for yourself until it is clearer.

Break it down into smaller parts if necessary.

STEP 2: LIST ALL POSSIBLE SOLUTIONS

Remember to include 'silly' or 'bad' suggestions, and as many ideas as you can.

STEP 3: LIST ADVANTAGES AND DISADVANTAGES

Highlight the pros and cons of each idea.

STEP 4: CHOOSE THE 'BEST' SOLUTION

Choose which idea you are going to try first.

Remember to take into account your resources:

- Time
- Money
- Skills
- Circumstances
- How will you carry it out?
- What problems might there be with it?
- How will you overcome them?
- Are there any bits you need to practise first?

STEP 5: REVIEW YOUR PROGRESS

Look at progress so far and revise your solution if necessary.

CHAPTER SUMMARY

- Problem-solving skills will help you deal with life situation difficulties and other problems such as mood difficulties.
- The first and most important step is to define the problems you may have at present.
- Going through the five-step process described above should help you find ways of solving problems.
- Reviewing your progress with the 'best' solution can help you learn how to deal with similar problems in the future.

11

Understanding sleep and sleep problems

This chapter aims to help you to understand:

- What sort of sleeping problems can be caused by chronic pain
- What kind of sleep pattern you have at present
- How much sleep you need
- How to use a sleep diary
- How to change unhelpful sleep habits

Problems with sleep usually fall into one of the following categories:

- Difficulty getting off to sleep
- Waking often, with problems dropping off again
- Waking in the early morning and being unable to sleep again
- Feeling tired, groggy and not refreshed on waking
- Sleeping too much or for too long

What sort of sleeping problems can be caused by chronic pain?

For people with chronic pain, there are some extra problems that can interfere with getting a good night's sleep.

Tick the ones that apply to you:

- It may be difficult to get comfortable or lie still for long.
- Being less active may lead to changes in sleep patterns.
- Some pain medication can make you drowsy during the day.
- Some people find that medications, which helped them to sleep at first, don't work in the long term.
- Some people feel that it's not worth sleeping longer because they have a 'hung-over' feeling the next day.
- Waking because of pain or nightmares can make you feel tense and makes it harder to get back to sleep.
- Some people get into the habit of napping during the day. This can be a way of finding some relief from the pain. However it can disrupt night-time sleep even more.
- At night, problems can seem worse because time seems to pass more slowly.
- Being worried or feeling low can affect sleeping patterns, whether you are in pain or not.
- Other problems or difficulties?

What kind of sleep pattern do you have at present?

Write down in your notebook what your sleep pattern is like now. Take last week as an example. (We will look at this in more detail later in this chapter.)

1 How many hours' sleep did you get, on average, at night?
2 How many hours' sleep did you get, on average, during the day?
3 Do you feel you are getting enough sleep?
4 What things affect how well you sleep? Use the problem list on the previous page for ideas, and add your own experiences.
5 What thoughts and worries do you have about your sleeping pattern?

Note: Discuss with your doctor any concerns you may have about your drugs and how they affect your sleep.

How much sleep do you need?

Adults never usually need more than 9 hours' sleep. Some people report feeling refreshed and alert after 5 hours. Generally, having one longer sleep is more satisfying than napping and waking often. People vary in how many hours' sleep they need. Your sleep requirements can also depend on your age, and on how active you are.

Our need for sleep decreases as we get older. For example:

* A teenager may need 10 hours' sleep.
* At age 40–60, we usually need 6–7 hours' sleep.
* At age 60 and older, we need only 5–6 hours' sleep.

If you are not active, you will need less sleep, but may feel more fatigue due to inactivity (see Chapter 9).

You may have a clear idea of how much sleep you should get. However, this may be based on what your sleep pattern used to be, rather than on what is happening now. A disrupted sleep pattern can usually be improved, despite ongoing pain. It is common for people who have trouble sleeping to feel edgy and irritable. Lack of sleep can affect your concentration. However, it is easy to let thoughts about poor sleep (for example, worrying that lack of sleep is causing you long-term harm) get out of proportion. (Take, for instance, **Jim's** worrying over Ann's health and all the things that he needs to do every day even when his pain is severe.) Sleeplessness is quite common, even for people who do not have ongoing pain problems. It does not usually cause harm.

You can do positive things to improve your sleeping pattern. Here are some ideas that have helped others with chronic pain to have better-quality sleep. They may help you improve your sleeping pattern too.

How to use a sleep diary

If you feel that you do not have a good sleep pattern, you could start keeping a Sleep Diary. For a whole week, write down all the times you were asleep, whether you meant to be or not. There is a Sleep Diary below, with an example.

It is important to write down even a five-minute snooze, because it can affect your sleep later. Keeping a Sleep Diary will give you a 'baseline' for your sleeping pattern, so that you can see if any changes that you make are working. Fill in the hours when you were asleep. You can then see what your sleep pattern is like. You can put in a note about where you were when you fell asleep (for example, if you dropped off in front of the TV).

Note down:

- When you took tablets which affect your sleep
- If you were worrying
- If you had a nightmare
- If you woke because of pain or discomfort

All this information will help to focus your efforts to get better-quality sleep.

Here is an example of **Jim's** sleep diary. The shaded areas are times spent sleeping.

How many hours of sleep is Jim getting each day, on average?

How does this number of hours compare with adequate sleep for you, given your age and activity level?

There is a blank Sleep Diary overleaf for you to use.

What did your Sleep Diary tell you about your sleep pattern?

How can you change unhelpful sleep habits?

Most people sleep better if they have a regular bedtime routine. Being 'in tune' with your 'biological clock' (which regulates your body's rhythms) can help you get more satisfying sleep. You will also be more alert when you are awake. Plan a regular time (preferably before midnight) when you will go to bed. Get up at the same time each day. This can be hard if you have been awake during the night. However, it is worth making the effort to get up at a regular time because, after a few days, it can make a real difference to your night-time sleep. If you do need to have a rest during the day, make sure it is not too late in the afternoon, and don't sleep for longer than an hour. If you sleep during the day, it will probably reduce the amount of sleep you get at night.

Time	Mon	Tue	Wed	Thu	Fri	Sat	Sun
6 a.m.							
7 a.m.							
8 a.m.							
9 a.m.							
10 a.m.							
11 a.m.							
12 p.m.							
1 p.m.							In the car
2 p.m.				1 hr in my chair			
3 p.m.							
4 p.m.	30 mins						
5 p.m.							
6 p.m.							
7 p.m.							
8 p.m.							
9 p.m.		Chair					
10 p.m.							
11 p.m.					11–30		
12 a.m.							
1 a.m.							
2 a.m.							
3 a.m.		3–15	No sleep	½hr			In chair
4 a.m.							
5 a.m.							

Sleep Diary

Fill this in for at least a week and make a note of:
- Where you were when you were asleep
- When you took drugs for pain or sleep
- Whether anything seemed to keep you awake
- Shade in the boxes for the hours when you were asleep

Time	Mon	Tue	Wed	Thu	Fri	Sat	Sun
6 a.m.							
7 a.m.							
8 a.m.							
9 a.m.							
10 a.m.							
11 a.m.							
12 p.m.							
1 p.m.							
2 p.m.							
3 p.m.							
4 p.m.							
5 p.m.							
6 p.m.							
7 p.m.							
8 p.m.							
9 p.m.							
10 p.m.							
11 p.m.							
12 a.m.							
1 a.m.							
2 a.m.							
3 a.m.							
4 a.m.							
5 a.m.							

TIPS ON PREPARING YOUR BEDROOM

Tick those ideas you might try:

- ❑ Try to make yourself as comfortable as possible.
- ❑ Getting a good mattress is important. Try to find one that gives you the right amount of support, not too soft or hard. If you have a saggy mattress, and cannot replace it yet, find a board to go under it. This will make it firm, but not too hard.
- ❑ Make the room comfortable, warm (but not too hot), and as quiet and dark as possible.
- ❑ Avoid watching television or videos in bed. This can be a difficult habit to break. If you do have problems sleeping, TV and interesting radio programmes tend to stimulate you to stay awake. Keep them for a different room, if possible, and definitely turn them off when you are going to bed.
- ❑ While you are working on a better sleeping routine, don't read interesting books and magazines in bed. Keep them in another room, to read during the day. All these things help to strengthen the connection between going to bed and sleeping.

TIPS ON DEVELOPING A BEDTIME ROUTINE

Tick those ideas you might try:

- ❑ Have a nice warm bath or shower before bed each night.
- ❑ Avoid having a heavy meal, but have a light snack if it helps.
- ❑ Having a warm milky drink or some herbal tea helps some people. You can even have a 'special' bedtime mug, which you keep as part of your bedtime routine.
- ❑ Coffee, tea and cola drinks with caffeine can keep you awake. The caffeine is a stimulant, which means it makes you more alert. Try not to have any of these after 6pm. You may want to work towards this gradually if you usually drink a lot of these in the evening.
- ❑ Make sure that you have drunk plenty of fluid during the day – ideally, eight tall glasses of clear water in total.

❑ Alcohol is also likely to interfere with healthy sleep. Try to drink other things in the evening, and not so much that you will need the bathroom too often!

❑ If you smoke, try to cut down cigarette-smoking in the evening. Nicotine is a stimulant, which again makes it harder to settle to sleep.

❑ If you do have medication to take at night, take it at the same time every evening as part of your routine.

❑ If you have any questions about how your tablets affect your sleep, write them down in your notebook. Discuss them at your next appointment with the doctor who prescribes them.

GENERAL TIPS TO IMPROVE SLEEP

Tick those ideas you might try:

❑ Regular exercise and activity (see Chapter 9) help to promote sleep. For maximum benefit, do your exercises earlier in the day, a few hours before bed. It can take a while to get ready for sleep after doing an exercise session.

❑ Relaxation exercises can help (see Chapter 12). These are best carried out earlier in the evening, before starting your bedtime routine. You can use a 'quick relaxation' if you feel tense when you go to bed.

❑ If you are concerned about disturbing a partner because you are restless, this can make you feel more tense. Try talking about it with them, if you have not done so already. For example, how much are you disturbing them? Do they mind? What would help? Would it be worth sleeping in separate rooms or separate beds for a while, until the problem has eased up? Are there any other possibilities that would work?

DEALING WITH WORRIES AND UNHELPFUL THOUGHTS

Tick those ideas you might try:

☐ It can be hard to put worries to one side. But if you find that you 'just lie there', with worries going round in your head, make a decision to worry about things the next day.

☐ Some people find that it helps to have a 'worry book' next to the bed, in which they can write down anything they need to deal with. This allows you to put worries to one side without feeling anxious about forgetting something that needs your attention the next day. The benefit is that you will be more alert during the day, and so more able to work towards solving problems.

☐ Some people find that it helps simply to have a 'worry half hour' during the day. This means having a time when you allow yourself to worry, leaving you free to get on with other things the rest of the day.

☐ 'Trying hard' to go to sleep can be unhelpful. Worrying about not being asleep keeps you awake! If you have done everything reasonable to prepare for sleep, you will at least be relatively relaxed and able to rest your body.

☐ You can also 'break the rules' if you choose to, for example, by having a drink, or watching TV in bed until far too late because it is an exciting film. However, if you coose to do this, you will need to accept that you may not sleep so well. It will have been 'worth it', so you won't worry about being awake, or feeling more tired the following day.

WHAT IF YOU NEED TO GET UP BECAUSE YOU CAN'T SLEEP, OR YOU HAVE WOKEN IN THE MIDDLE OF THE NIGHT AND CAN'T GET BACK TO SLEEP?

Tick those ideas you might try:

☐ Go into a different room, and keep the lights fairly low.
☐ Do something unexciting.
☐ Remember to use your notebook to keep a quick note of things that are worrying you.

❑ Leave trying to solve things until the morning. You will be more able to deal with things during the day.

❑ If you read, choose something that is not too interesting or too much hard work. If you listen to music, choose something calming.

❑ If you have a drink, avoid caffeine.

❑ Get your body into the habit of using night-time for sleeping. At times when you want to be asleep, avoid stimulating your mind and body.

❑ Go back to bed when you feel sleepy. Even if you have been awake for some time in the night, try to get up at the same time each day, at least until you have established a better sleeping pattern.

❑ Practise your relaxation skills (see Chapter 12).

THINGS TO DO TO IMPROVE YOUR SLEEPING PATTERNS

Tick those ideas you want to do or try:

❑ Have a regular bedtime.

❑ Have a regular 'bedtime routine'.

❑ Have a light snack/milky drink if you want to.

❑ Have your 'special mug'!

❑ Go to bed before midnight.

❑ Prepare for bed.

❑ Make the room and bed as comfortable as possible.

❑ Have a firm mattress with a soft foam or mattress pad on top.

❑ Have a relaxing bath/shower.

❑ Put worries to one side, to deal with during the day.

❑ Have a 'worry'/'things to remember' book handy.

❑ Exercise during the day.

❑ Relaxation sessions in the day.

❑ Get up rather than lie there too long, e.g after 15 minutes.

❑ Do something uninteresting if awake in the night, e.g read something 'light'/listen to something calming.

❑ Go back to bed when sleepy.

❑ Keep the bedroom for sleeping (and sex).

❑ Have a regular getting-up time.

❑ Discuss the side-effects of medications with your doctor if necessary.

THINGS NOT TO DO TO IMPROVE YOUR SLEEPING PATTERNS

Tick those things to stop or change:

- ❑ 'Nap' during the day.
- ❑ Eat a heavy meal.
- ❑ Drink alcohol.
- ❑ Drink coffee/tea/cola drinks (containing caffeine) or smoke.
- ❑ Watch TV in bed.
- ❑ Listen to interesting music.
- ❑ Read anything stimulating in bed.
- ❑ Try hard to go to sleep (even try staying awake instead!).
- ❑ Worry about not being asleep.
- ❑ Try to solve problems or make plans.
- ❑ Exercise just before bed.
- ❑ Do a deep relaxation session at bedtime.
- ❑ Sleep in a chair (see Jim's sleep diary).

CHAPTER SUMMARY

- Sleep problems are very common, especially in chronic pain conditions. Sleep patterns *can* change for the better.
- Using a sleep diary can help you understand your own sleeping pattern. It helps to be clear about what the problems are, and where to start making changes.
- There are many suggestions on improving your sleep pattern and how to prepare for a good night's sleep.

12

Relaxation

This chapter aims to help you understand more about:

- What relaxation is
- How relaxation can help with chronic pain
- What can help you relax
- How to practise relaxing
- What can make it difficult to relax

What is relaxation?

Relaxation doesn't mean simply sitting still and doing nothing. You can be very tense while sitting still. For instance, you could be watching a horror movie on TV, or you could be thinking about the frustrations of the day.

When you relax, the tension in your muscles is reduced. Reducing tension in the muscles can make you feel calm and comfortable. Relaxation also means allowing the mind to become less active, giving it a break, slowing down fast thoughts. Relaxation skills can be really useful for anyone, but particularly for people who are living with long-term pain.

TABLE 12.1: HOW DO YOU KNOW WHEN YOU'RE RELAXED?

What do you notice about yourself when you feel relaxed?	What do you notice about yourself when you feel stressed or worried?
Tick those that apply to you:	Tick those that apply to you:
Warm	Shallow, fast breathing
Heavy or light	Muscular tension
Slow, controlled breathing	'Clouded' mind
Less muscular tension	Poor concentration and memory
Clearer mind, more alert	Difficulty making decisions
Good concentration and memory	More pain
Less pain	Racing or repeated thoughts
Mood – lighter and brighter	Mood – low or worried moods
Others? _____	Others? _____

How can relaxation help with chronic pain?

When muscles are tense, it can cause pain, or make existing pain worse. For instance, many people find that their shoulders or neck hurt after a stressful day. This pain is probably mainly due to tense muscles and altered body positions.

When pain is severe, it is natural to tense up in response to it. Learning to notice tension early, and reduce it, can be very useful. Being relaxed will help you manage pain more successfully. Relaxation can give you a break from tension in the middle of a difficult day. It can remind you not to rush or 'overdo it' and to use pacing skills (see Chapter 8).

Relaxation is a skill that does take a bit of practice to learn. Some people find it easier than others. However, relaxing is something positive you can do, even in the middle of a severe setback (see Chapter 16). It may even make flare-ups less likely to happen, and less intense when they do. It can be seen as another tool in your kit of coping skills to help you manage pain more successfully.

What can help you relax?

Here are a few things that can help you to relax.
Tick those you might like to try:

❑ Simple breathing patterns
❑ Exercise programmes, such as Yoga, T'ai Chi or Pilates
❑ Concentrating on reducing tension in various parts of the body
❑ Self-hypnosis
❑ Sitting in a beautiful garden, smelling the flowers
❑ Imagining pleasant images or pictures
❑ Listening to a relaxation tape
❑ Listening to a favourite piece of music
❑ Attending a local relaxation group
❑ Being somewhere comfortable
❑ Recorded sounds from nature, such as the sound of the sea or birds singing
❑ Focusing on a candle or looking at a simple picture
❑ Pleasant smells, such as aromatherapy oils

WHAT MAKES YOU FEEL RELAXED?

Write or draw your ideas in your notebook.

How to practise relaxing

Two useful approaches are described below.

Time out relaxation

For a 'time out' relaxation session, set aside about 20–30 minutes. Making time to practise and focus on relaxing will help you learn how to relax fully and deeply. When you first learn a relaxation technique, being in a quiet, comfortable place can help. Lie down on a bed or mat, or sit in your most comfortable chair. Try to find a time when you are unlikely to be disturbed. If you wish, a partner or friend could do the exercise with you. Or you may prefer to do it alone. Listening to a recording or going to a class can be called 'time out' relaxation. There are lots of relaxation tapes or CD roms available to buy. (Note: If you plan to use a relaxation tape, don't use it while driving or operating machinery!) Try and look at your relaxation sessions as part of your treatment, in the same way as a daily exercise programme.

QUICK RELAXATION

As well as using a 'time out' technique, you can start to use relaxation in everyday situations. As soon as you notice any tension in your muscles, practise letting go of the tension, and relaxing. When you have had a bit more practice, you can use relaxation and breathing in more stressful situations – for instance, when you feel angry or frustrated.

You can also practise 'scanning'. This means checking your body for tension by noticing your feet, your legs, your knees, your hips, your abdomen, your chest, your shoulders, your neck, your head, your face and your jaw. As you notice any tension, let it go.

You can also observe your breathing, and remember to breathe calmly and comfortably.

You can use 'reminders' – for example, put a sticker on the fridge or on your mirror, and check for tension each time you see the sticker.

What can make it difficult to practise relaxation?

It can be difficult to make time to practise relaxation without being disturbed. If you have a lot of demands on your time, you may need to be creative about when and how to do relaxation. You may feel like the sort of person who 'just can't relax'. However, there is usually a way round these obstacles.

You can use problem-solving skills (see Chapter 10) to help you overcome barriers. Here are some ideas that might be helpful:

- You could make a regular appointment with yourself at a certain time of day.
- Let others know that you are not available at that time.
- Unplug your phone, or leave the answer machine on.
- Notice times in the day when you are least busy, or when people are least likely to call – try using those times for your relaxation session.
- Perhaps you could make space when your children have gone to school, or your partner has gone out.
- You could practise your relaxation skills in the evening when you are by yourself.
- Remind others (and yourself!), if you need to, that this is a daily treatment. You are not 'being lazy'.
- If you find yourself feeling guilty about taking time out, check out unhelpful thoughts (see Chapter 14).

When getting ready to listen to a relaxation tape, try to make sure the lights are not too bright, and the temperature suits you. It may be difficult to find a position to lie down or sit comfortably. But this does not mean that you can't benefit from the relaxation. At first, as soon as you start, you may want to fidget or cough, or you may get an itch or a fit of giggles. If so, feel free to change position, scratch or laugh! Use breathing exercises as a guide. On relaxation tapes or CD roms, you are often asked to breathe deeply and evenly. Remember that you do not have to hold your breath to wait for the next instruction.

Some people find that they have odd thoughts or images going through their minds when they start to learn to relax. This is quite normal and happens to most people. However, if you get a lot of really distressing thoughts or images after trying an exercise a few times, talk to the person who gave you the information about it. There is usually a way to overcome such experiences.

Some people find that they fall asleep before the end of a session. This is not a problem, but, with more practice, you will probably find that you don't fall asleep. Then you will feel even more relaxed and refreshed at the end of the session.

Relaxation exercises can be fun, as well as helping you manage pain. They can give you a feeling of well-being and alertness without tension.

IS THERE ANYONE WHO SHOULD NOT DO RELAXATION EXERCISES?

Nearly everybody can benefit from some form of relaxation exercise. However, you should seek advice from a health professional before you do a new relaxation exercise. This is particularly important if you have:

- An acute medical condition
- A history of severe mental illness, such as psychosis
- Untreated Post-Traumatic Stress Disorder

If you have any questions, write them down in your note-book for when you next see your therapist or healthcare professional.

CHAPTER SUMMARY

- Relaxation means being able to reduce bodily tension and stressful thinking.
- Relaxation can help with chronic pain and tension by helping to loosen the muscles and joints. It also helps to 'unwind' the mind.
- There are different ways of relaxing, including Time out relaxation and Quick relaxation.
- It helps if you can deal with obstacles to relaxation before starting your relaxation session.

13

Pain, communication and relationships

This chapter aims to help you to understand:

- How close relationships can be affected by pain
- How to manage difficulties in relationships
- How to change behavior
- How to communicate and share your concerns
- How to deal with sexual problems
- How to make sexual relationships easier

ADVICE ON USING THIS CHAPTER

This chapter is divided into Part 1 ('Communication and Sharing Concerns') and Part 2 ('Chronic Pain and Sexual Relationships'). You can make use of whichever parts of this chapter you feel are relevant to you. You might want to read it with a partner, or leave it for them to read by themselves. You could also show them the other chapters that you have worked through, such as Chapter 1.

PART 1: COMMUNICATION AND SHARING CONCERNS

How close relationships can be affected by pain

Pain has an effect on people around the person with chronic pain. For example, you might find yourself saying 'ouch' or wincing when you see someone else twist his or her ankle. People usually 'feel for' the person who is feeling pain, and will often try to help.

Sometimes, people feel closer because they are facing problems together. But sometimes communication becomes more difficult, or even breaks down. Family, friends or partners might be concerned about you. People close to you might know exactly when you need help, when you need to be left alone and when you need to talk. Or it may sometimes seem as if sympathy has run out. You might feel that they have never really understood how your pain condition affects you.

For a short while, being looked after can help, for example, when you have a severe setback. But friends or family members may try to do too much for you. And after a while, if you are 'looked after' all the time, it can make it harder to feel in control of your situation or that you have a useful role to play at home or in life.

It can be hard to talk clearly about your feelings or thoughts, especially if you are feeling frustrated, anxious or depressed. Pain can make it harder to make the effort to go out and be with people. Withdrawing from others is a common response to chronic pain and it can be a helpful coping method. However it may also become an unhelpful habit. If used too much, it can lead to isolation and loneliness.

Learning to communicate or talk about what is helpful to you, saying 'no' and negotiating compromises and solutions are all very useful skills. And they are needed even more if you are managing chronic pain.

Think about your present situation. Do you:

- Feel as if others just don't understand what you need?
- Find it hard to say 'no' when you want to?
- Find it hard to ask for help?
- Find that other people tend to do 'too much' for you?
- Want to be able to negotiate better or compromise more?
- Feel that other people's compassion or sympathy has run out?
- Withdraw from social situations or activities more?
- Feel like your role at home or at work has been taken away or undermined?

Some families talk about these things openly, and are good at finding compromises or solutions that work for them. For others, talking about emotions or thoughts does not come easily. Maybe they have never tried it, or it has not seemed necessary or important before now.

Talking to each other can be more difficult when there is a person in the family who has long-term pain. Perhaps there is a fear of hurting the other person's feelings, or starting another row? Either way, it can be difficult for all the people involved.

Many people with chronic pain say they have become more irritable since the pain started. They also report becoming depressed or angry or worried more easily. Sometimes all these moods occur together. At a time when you most need to be close to people around you, being irritable can get in the way. Sometimes, getting angry with yourself for being short-tempered makes it even harder to deal with frustrations and solve problems.

Steve described his situation like this:

. . . My partner Nicole is a very caring person. She would do anything for anyone, especially me. Since I've been in so much pain, I seem to bite her head off for helping. Then I get so angry with myself for shouting, and then feel too cross with myself to ask for help when I need it. I never had so much trouble talking with her before . . .

One person may assume that the other doesn't want to talk. The partner or family member may think that he or she knows what the person with the pain is thinking because they know that person well. But this type of attempted 'mind reading' can often lead to difficulties, conflict or misunderstandings.

Sometimes the family members or partner don't know how to help. They may be coping with many changes in their partner, parent, or son or daughter because of their pain. These changes could include:

- The loss of the person as they used to know them
- The loss of doing things together
- The person in pain having a lot of mood swings
- Things having to be done differently about the house or at work
- Changed finances
- Changed roles
- Getting less help
- Doing more at home
- Having to work different hours or having to give up work

- Having to get up at night to care for the children
- Needing to plan outings more carefully
- Feeling a general sense of loss because expectations of the future have changed

It can be hard to cope with the distress of a person you are very close to, or whom you care about a lot, when they experience periods of severe pain. You may feel powerless, especially when it is difficult to talk about these issues.

If you are the person in pain and your mood is low, or you seem irritable, other people may feel hurt, or even rejected. They might feel that their efforts to help are not working. And they may give up on inviting you out, because you have said 'no' several times. Most of these problems can be eased by talking about them openly. If you need to talk things through, try to choose a time when you are not likely to have extra pressures or interruptions. If it seems difficult for both partners to feel listened to, it can help to agree to listen carefully without interrupting for five minutes, and then let the other person do the same. (For more ideas, see Chapter 10 on problem-solving.)

It is hard to cope with the impact of pain, and the many changes it can bring. It may seem as if you are losing control of many parts of your life. However, becoming aware of what is happening is the first step in learning to cope with chronic pain and its effects.

How to manage difficulties in relationships

In Chapter 2 ('Understanding Chronic Pain and Pain Systems'), pain was described as an individual, 'subjective' experience. This means that no one can know exactly what your pain experience is like. However, you can tell others what body sensations you are feeling, such as pressure or tightness. You can also share how the pain makes you feel in terms of your mood, such as fed up, worried and so on.

People will see how you behave and try to understand these actions. For instance, you might grit your teeth, limp, rub the painful area, withdraw to bed, moan, or be snappy and short-tempered. These are 'pain behaviors', which communicate something to those around you. People can be very sympathetic and supportive, especially in the short term (for example, if you fall and hurt your arm and have elbow pain for several weeks).

In the long term, all but the most 'saintly' can run out of sympathy or patience with persisting pain. This is when a different approach can help. People close to you need to understand what you are trying to achieve. Otherwise, they can sometimes jump to the wrong conclusions, which can be unhelpful. It helps to explain clearly how you plan to manage your day or week and your pain.

Then they can:

- Encourage you, and help to reward your efforts (see Chapter 7).
- Help you to stick at it when the going gets tough.
- Remind you to 'pace' yourself and your activities (see Chapter 8).
- Learn to avoid being over-protective towards you.
- Stop doing things for you that you *could* do yourself, given time and encouragement.
- Learn to encourage you for trying to stick to your plan.

If you are close to someone who wants to help, have a talk about what your goals are. Talk about the helpful ways to achieve them (see Chapter 6).

Write in your notebook what goals you are trying to achieve that you would like to share with _____ (name).

How to change behavior

It's well known that if children are rewarded for an action they are more likely to repeat it. Think about this in relation to yourself. If you are rewarded for a particular behavior, you are also more likely to do that behavior again. Unfortunately, this principle applies to unhelpful as well as helpful behaviors.

Let's take an example:

Imagine that you want to get out to the local shop to buy bread and a newspaper. You have chronic pain, which makes you stiff and tired in the morning. Someone who loves you will always offer to do it for you if you tell them that the pain is bad today.

What are the results?

- You get the paper and the bread every day.
- You do not get encouragement to do it for yourself.
- You feel more 'dependent' on someone else.
- Your self-esteem is lower, you don't feel 'in control', you lose confidence.
- What else might you lose?

The end result is that you are 'rewarded' for saying that you are in pain. The long-term effect on your feelings, pain and behavior is not always helpful.

Let's imagine a different scene:

You want to get the bread and the paper from the shop every day. You have chronic pain and you are very stiff in a morning so it is hard to get started. You set yourself a pacing baseline. You plan it so that you can get to the shop if you rest on the bench for two minutes on the way there **and** again on the way back. Someone who loves you will always offer to do it for you if you say that the pain is bad today. You explain to them that it would help to have a reward, such as a cup of tea, when you get back from the shop. It would also help if they said 'well done' or 'thanks!' to you, so focusing on your achievements despite the pain and stiffness. You ask them to encourage you to go, especially when you don't feel like it, or you are having a bad day.

What are the results?

- You get the bread and the paper every day.
- You get the satisfaction of achieving it yourself, using your own plan and your pacing skills.
- You get a 'reward', which helps you to improve things.
- Your loved one gets to see you working through the problem and knows what will *really* help *you*.
- You feel more independent and more in control, and you gain confidence.
- You are managing your pain better.

Furthermore . . .

Your family, or the people close to you, now understand that you are not doing any further harm by starting to exercise and getting active. And you are not 'slacking' when you slow down, pace yourself, take a break before the job is finished and give yourself a reward for trying.

It is more helpful to be allowed to do things at your own pace, rather than have someone else do them for you. They can then help you with things that you really can't manage, such as heavy lifting.

How to communicate and share your concerns

Talking about living with pain is quite difficult at times. Using the questions below may help you, your partner or your family to understand better how to manage the pain and have better times.

- What is the hardest thing about living with chronic pain?
- What do I/we do that makes it easier for you to manage your pain?
- What do I/we do that makes it harder to manage your pain?
- What can I/we do to help that we are not doing now?

You could write the answers, and any ideas that come up, in your notebook.

With practice, you can learn to tell your loved ones what will help you to manage your pain better. For instance, if those around you pay attention to your pain (perhaps by asking, 'How is your neck?'), this can focus your thoughts on it more of the time. In fact, it can make the pain seem worse. People *want* to help, and don't usually want others to suffer. This can sometimes lead to well-meaning concern and being over-protective.

It can help to 'challenge your own negative thoughts' or be aware of unhelpful thinking. Try this when you realize that you or the other person may be 'mind reading'. If this causes difficulties, then challenge these negative thoughts. This may help improve your moods (see Chapter 14) and ability to communicate with others.

The following suggestions may help those around you to give you the right kind of support. Ask them to tick those suggestions they think they could try:

❑ Understand the difference between chronic and acute pain systems in the body.

❑ Encourage and support you to keep going on your pain management plan.

❑ Notice when you are trying to cope better.

❑ Remember *not* to ask you how the pain is (it makes you focus attention on it).

❑ Remind you of your day-to-day success in achieving your goals.

❑ Only offer help when you ask for it, or when you have agreed it is part of your pain management plan.

❑ Reward you or do something pleasurable when you are trying.

❑ Do problem-solving with you.

❑ Know that you are not doing further harm by getting active.

❑ Know that you are not exaggerating or being lazy when you take rest breaks and 'pace' yourself.

❑ Know that you can support, encourage and listen to them, even if you are in pain.

Try different suggestions and work out which ones are most helpful for you and others close to you. You can experiment several times with these suggestions or your own ideas. See what helps to improve relationships, and makes you feel more confident and supported. Experimenting also means discovering what does *not* help communication and relationships, which is valuable in itself. And remember to reward yourself and your partner and family when your efforts prove successful.

PART 2: CHRONIC PAIN AND SEXUAL RELATIONSHIPS

If you have a partner, being faced with so many challenges means that you need to be close and intimate, perhaps even more than before. Being in pain, or being afraid to cause the other person harm, can lead people to avoid physical intimacy. But in chronic pain conditions it's important to realize that you can have a physical relationship that works for you as a couple.

This information on sexual relationships is aimed at heterosexual couples, but single people or gay couples may also find it useful. Organizations, such as Relate, will also provide reading materials, confidential help and advice on sexual and relationship issues (see Useful Information at the back of this book).

How to deal with sexual problems

Many people with chronic pain and their partners have sexual problems. Sometimes problems begin because of the pain (for example, when the person doesn't seem interested in sex, or because the partner is fearful of causing pain or being hurt). Sometimes pain makes existing problems worse.

If these issues are dealt with, sex can help maintain closeness and relax both of you. It can also reduce stress and relieve pain. Pain does not make you asexual. The drive is still there – it may be even stronger. Being in pain does not mean you do not have all the parts in working order! One way of dealing with problems is to avoid sex altogether. However this can be upsetting and can add to a couple's problems, especially if they find it difficult to talk it over.

Avoiding sexual activity can also lead to avoidance of all physical closeness. For **Jim and Ann**, this was distressing for both of them, especially at a time when Ann needed to feel much closer to Jim. So not dealing with the problem can leave sex as an area of tension and anxiety. This tension and worry may increase pain. Feelings of failure, frustration and guilt can become reasons for avoiding sexual activity. People often worry about their partner's sexual needs and whether not having sex is likely to cause problems in the relationship.

Many couples have full and contented lives without sexual intercourse. However, if you want to make changes, it will take understanding, time and commitment to deal with it, rather than avoid the problem. Firstly, both partners need to talk, perhaps several times. It is important to remember that it is a shared problem. Your partner needs to know your thoughts and feelings, so that you both understand exactly what is going on for each other.

For example, your partner may not understand that, even though it is difficult at the moment, you may want to make love in the future, in another few weeks.

Case history: Steve and Nicole

As Steve spent more time sleeping in the spare room, often six nights a week, Nicole thought he was no longer interested in their sex life. She already felt upset about a great many changes so trying to talk about the loss of making love seemed a real challenge. She did try to share her views and feelings when Steve was having a better day with less pain. He was a bit irritable about it as they talked it over. But he began to see what was concerning Nicole and they shared their feelings and thoughts slowly. Nicole discovered that Steve still found her very attractive and she realized the stress of making love was making Steve very anxious on top of more pain. Steve was keen to see if they could pace just being close together, touching and hugging more often and maybe sleep together more, two extra nights a week. Steve would also do some gentle stretches for his legs and back before cuddling Nicole in bed. Nicole was willing to try, and happier that they had started to share their feelings and thoughts.

Acknowledging both partners' feelings is an important part of keeping the connection strong between you.

How to make sexual relationships easier

PACING

Here are some tips for pacing your sexual relationship:

- It's important not to overdo it (either physically or emotionally) to start with.
- Start slowly: set a time together, if it helps you to relax.
- Just try kissing and cuddling, to begin with.
- Both partners need to understand and agree what is OK at this point. This can help to reduce anxiety and fear about increasing pain (for both partners).
- Set some goals: explore your sexuality together within agreed limits – taking it one step at a time.
- Full sexual intercourse is not necessarily the long-term goal for everyone.
- Practise!! Some couples find that one or both partners have arousal problems due to lack of practise. Frequent successful practise increases confidence, especially if both partners agree that there will be no pressure to 'perform'.

Pain does not need to be a reason for avoiding a sexual relationship. A couple can become more confident by touching and fondling. With some experimenting and a sense of humour, most couples can work out satisfactory positions that will not cause pain.

THOUGHTS AND FEELINGS

Sex in a loving mutual relationship cannot cause harm to any part of the body. However, like exercising, for the first few times there may be a temporary increase in pain.

Negative thoughts can make it harder to relax and enjoy sex. For example:

- *I know I am going to suffer from this, it will be dreadful.*
- *How can I stop this?*
- *I must satisfy her/him this time/always.*
- *I must be the active one.*
- *I should always be willing.*
- *I can't deal with this demand on me, it is too much.*

If you find yourself thinking negative thoughts, get your partner to challenge them with you, so you have a more balanced view about being physically closer and sexually active. For example, **Jim and Ann** shared their concerns, including Jim's prediction about how he would suffer awful pain if Ann touched him around his chest. Jim realized that Ann enjoyed some massage with her favourite oils and it was pleasurable for both of them. They found experimenting in this way helped. Jim was much less fearful when he realized he did not have to suffer being touched in his sensitive pain areas.

Sexual relationships are more than just intercourse, and there are many alternative ways of being intimate. For instance, many couples find comfort and reassurance lying together, caressing each other, taking a shower together, or massaging each other in favourite places. Physical satisfaction can be gained from stimulation or masturbating, stroking or kissing. No harm will occur if both partners find this emotionally and physically acceptable.

COMFORTABLE POSITIONS FOR SEXUAL INTERCOURSE

Old positions may not work for you if you have pain. Here are some suggestions to try.

- Be honest and open with each other about your feelings.
- Remember your sense of humour, experiment and take it slowly. You will find out what works for you both.
- Lying-on-the-side positions are very good for the woman, and can be very comfortable for the man.
- The woman may find it more comfortable to have both legs over the man's top leg.
- It is often best for the person in pain to let their partner take the dominant position on top and do the moving.

There are pictures of helpful positions for sex in the Appendix on page 297.

CHAPTER SUMMARY

- Chronic pain affects relationships and it's important to talk through these effects on those people who are close to you.
- Pain may have caused many losses in your life. This can have many effects on your moods and on those who are close to you.
- It's possible to change some of these problems in relationships. Knowing how to talk things through can help you make changes to adapt or cope better. It can be helpful to focus on successes, achievements and enjoyable times, rather than on the pain itself.
- Sexual problems can be eased by experimenting, by pacing sexual activity, by challenging unhelpful thoughts and feelings, and by finding comfortable positions for sexual intercourse.

14

Managing depression, anxiety and anger

This chapter aims to help you understand:

> - What moods can happen with chronic pain
> - More about moods, such as depression and guilt, anxiety, worry and fear, anger and frustration
> - How to manage these moods in helpful ways by using a Thought Challenge Worksheet

What moods can occur because of pain?

The most common moods that occur because of chronic pain are:

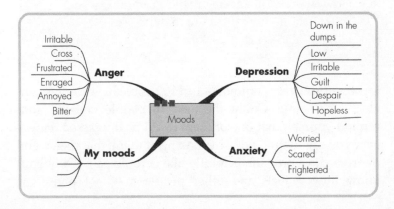

Circle those moods on the previous page that you feel are linked with your pain problem, and add your own mood experiences.

Pain is not just a physical event. It affects:

- Our moods and emotions or feelings
- Our thinking about ourselves, other people and the future
- The things we do or stop doing (our behaviors)
- Our relationships with others, including partner, family and friends

This chapter is divided into Part 1 ('Managing Depression'), Part 2 ('Managing Anxiety') and Part 3 ('Managing Anger').

PART 1: MANAGING DEPRESSION

This section aims to help you understand:

- Why people become depressed with chronic pain
- How depression affects people's thinking
- What factors can contribute to depression
- How to manage depression

Depression is very common – 1 in 10 people have depression at any one time. Count the next 10 people you see and remind yourself that one of them could be depressed. However you might not know, by looking at them, that they were depressed. Depression is a little like chronic pain. Only **you** know how it feels and other people may not notice or understand it. If they *do* notice, what they may see is a quieter, more withdrawn person who seems:

- To laugh less
- To be tearful sometimes, or look or sound tired
- Be forgetful or lacking in concentration
- Unwilling to do things or join in with others
- To lack confidence
- To be less interested in sex or intimacy
- To feel guilty and low
- To be negative or pessimistic, sometimes hopeless, about the future

If you experience any of these changes yourself for two weeks or longer, then you may have depression.

Why do people become depressed with chronic pain?

Persistent pain is very stressful and exhausting. Feelings of helplessness and frustration can contribute to low mood. Sleep patterns are upset. Tiredness can set in and this too can lower mood. There are many changes and losses, such as work or friends, or being less active and able to do things with others.

How depression affects people's thinking

Depression in chronic pain can cause specific changes in how people think, leading to a negative 'chain reaction':

Lack of control over the pain, especially at times of severe pain, increases my belief that I am helpless.

Then I overestimate my physical disability.

Which then causes catastrophic thoughts about what is happening and what will happen to me.

↓

So I become pessimistic and at times see my future as hopeless.

What factors can contribute to depression?

Tick any factors that you feel are important for you:

- ❑ Life events
- ❑ Financial difficulties
- ❑ Bereavements
- ❑ Relationship difficulties
- ❑ Work stresses

UNHELPFUL BEHAVIORS

Reduced levels of physical activity and ability to do things, e.g. driving, gardening

Drinking too much alcohol, or using drugs like heroin or cocaine

LOSSES, SUCH AS

Your job

Some of your friends

Some of your family members
Your role or main purpose in life
Your health
Your plans or goals in life, especially future goals

OTHER PROBLEMS

Lack of sleep and frequent tiredness
Side-effects from medicines for pain-relief or lowering blood pressure (e.g. beta-blockers)
Changes in your thinking that become extreme and negative
Others? _____

If you are depressed, write in your notebook any factors that you think may be linked to your own depressed mood.

Depression can affect all five 'parts' of the person: their thinking, moods, behaviors, their body symptoms and their current life situation. This is shown in the person-centred model on the opposite page.

Add any additional symptoms you may have to this person-centred model.

The person-centred model can help you to see how to change your moods. Changing one part can enable the other parts to change. For example, if sleep is a problem, improving it may make you feel more energetic (**body symptom**) and more enthusiastic (**mood**). You may be able to do a few more activities at home with family or friends (**behavior**). You might then think: 'I am glad I can do this and the family are supportive' (**more positive thinking**).

The person-centred model on the next page shows the impact of chronic pain on **Maria**, her life, her moods, thoughts and behaviors. For example, it shows Maria:

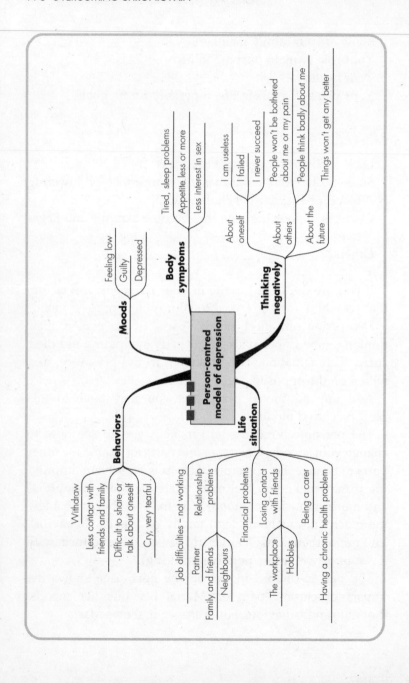

Person-centred model of depression

Moods
- Feeling low
- Guilty
- Depressed

Body symptoms
- Tired, sleep problems
- Appetite less or more
- Less interest in sex

Thinking negatively
- About oneself
  - I am useless
  - I failed
  - I never succeed
- About others
  - People won't be bothered about me or my pain
  - People think badly about me
- About the future
  - Things won't get any better

Behaviors
- Withdraw
- Less contact with friends and family
- Difficult to share or talk about oneself
- Cry, very tearful

Life situation
- Job difficulties – not working
- Relationship problems
  - Partner
  - Family and friends
  - Neighbours
- Financial problems
- Losing contact with friends
  - The workplace
  - Hobbies
- Being a carer
- Having a chronic health problem

- Not doing activities with and for other people
- Several life situation factors that play a part in her depression (for example, being stuck at home all the time)

This model shows the link between Maria's chronic pain and her depression. (See page 201.) It helps to see possible areas to lessen and manage depression.

HOW UNHELPFUL THOUGHTS ARE LINKED TO DEPRESSION AND CHRONIC PAIN

In any situation, people try to make sense of what is happening by asking, 'Why me?' or 'What if . . .?' With chronic pain, your thoughts or beliefs about yourself, your illness and your health, and your ability to cope, may all be challenged. When people with chronic pain are depressed, they sometimes:

- Think they are useless or not needed
- Make assumptions about what others might think about them and their pain problem
- Have thoughts like 'I am helpless' about their pain control and their situation
- Avoid being with others

In depression, people frequently have negative and pessimistic thoughts. They also often find they have more memories of difficult and negative experiences, rather than pleasant or positive ones.

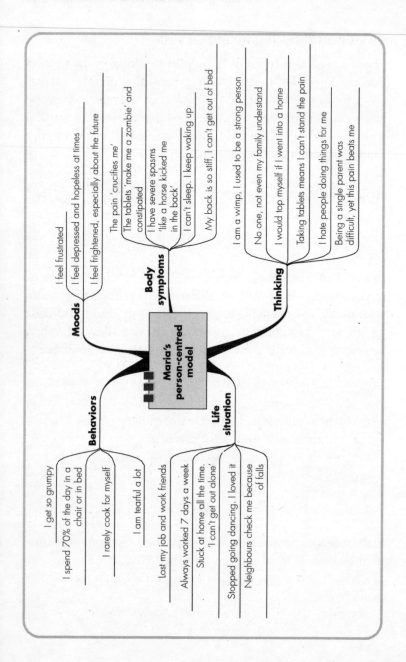

Maria's person-centred model

Moods
- I feel frustrated
- I feel depressed and hopeless at times
- I feel frightened, especially about the future

Body symptoms
- The pain 'crucifies me'
- The tablets 'make me a zombie' and constipated
- I have severe spasms 'like a horse kicked me in the back'
- I can't sleep. I keep waking up
- My back is so stiff, I can't get out of bed

Thinking
- I am a wimp, I used to be a strong person
- No one, not even my family understand
- I would top myself if I went into a home
- Taking tablets means I can't stand the pain
- I hate people doing things for me
- Being a single parent was difficult, yet this pain beats me

Behaviors
- I get so grumpy
- I spend 70% of the day in a chair or in bed
- I rarely cook for myself
- I am tearful a lot

Life situation
- Lost my job and work friends
- Always worked 7 days a week
- Stuck at home all the time. 'I can't get out alone'
- Stopped going dancing. I loved it
- Neighbours check me because of falls

Unhelpful thinking in depression

There are certain types of unhelpful thinking in depression that are particularly negative, keep repeating themselves and seem totally believable at the time. For example, someone having a difficult day with pain levels may start to think 'I feel useless.' This thought can then lead on to another thought: 'I am a useless person.'

TABLE 14.1: UNHELPFUL THINKING

Style of thinking	Typical statements
Making extreme statements/rules	I use extreme words like 'always', 'never' and 'typical' to summarize things. I make a lot of rules, using words like 'must', 'should', 'ought to' or 'got to'.
Personalization	I take the blame if and when things go wrong.
Bearing all responsibility	I take responsibility for things that are not totally my fault like whether everyone else has a good time.
Bias against myself	I overlook my strengths. I focus on my weaknesses. I downplay my achievements. I am my own worst critic.
Putting a negative view on things	I tend to focus on the negative in situations.
Negative mental filter	I have a gloomy view of the future. I make negative predictions about the future.
Catastrophic thinking	I predict that things will go wrong. I predict that the very worst events will happen. I predict the pain will be worse, whatever I do.
Mind reading	I 'mind read' what others think of me/how others see me. I often think that others don't like me/think badly of me.

This example shows how a person can draw conclusions based on how they feel, rather than on the actual situation. This type of extreme thinking or belief on a high pain level day can easily make you feel depressed.

ACTION 1: IDENTIFYING UNHELPFUL THINKING STYLES

Think about the last time your mood changed and you felt depressed or low. Recall what went through your mind and in the right hand column of the table below circle the unhelpful thoughts that you noticed.

ACTION 2: UNDERSTANDING HOW TO CHALLENGE UNHELPFUL THOUGHTS

When you feel unpleasant moods or emotions, notice what you are thinking.

Ask yourself: 'What went through my mind as I started to feel down or depressed?'

Moods can be affected by what you are thinking, and what you believe, about a situation. The table below shows an example of how thoughts and beliefs affected Maria's mood. When Maria noticed the unhelpful thoughts that had occurred during her mood change she realized she had been biased against herself, and her thinking style had been extreme, black and white, 'all or nothing'. She decided to challenge these unhelpful thoughts in Steps D and E (see the 'Challenging Thoughts Worksheet' on p. 207).

The effect of looking for a realistic response on Maria's mood was that she then assessed herself as feeling more cheerful, less sad and more hopeful.

TABLE 14.2: MARIA'S THOUGHTS AND MOODS

Step A: Event/situation	Step B – I tell myself . . . (Thoughts)	Step C – I feel and do something (Mood, Body sensations, Behaviors)	Step D – Thought challenge (I ask some useful, realistic questions)	Step E – Alternative realistic, balanced responses
Thinking 'I'd like to go out shopping but can't because of my pain; I'm at home, in the kitchen, on my own, sitting at the table.	What went through my mind as I started to feel low? I can't get out alone, so it's the same four walls. I don't want to be a wimp. I used to be a strong person. I have lost my job and the company of my work friends. **My belief about myself:** I am a wimp, a failure.	**Mood:** I feel depressed and hopeless. Mood level: 6/10 (0/10 = no depression 10/10 = very depressed). **Body sensations:** Back pain felt worse, with a burning feeling. **Behaviors:** Stopped eating; burst into tears.	1. Does it make sense to tell myself that I am a wimp?	1. I have tried to get going this morning and the pain is very severe. That doesn't mean I am failing just because I am having a difficult day. I am disappointed not to go out to the shops. It does not mean it is terrible.

2. Does it really mean I am a failure if I don't get out of the house today because of the pain and stiffness?

2. If I do fail to get out, it doesn't reflect on me as a person. I can fail to do things somedays without being 'a failure'. In future, when I think like that, I will tell myself that I have worked hard. I can only do my best at the time.

HOW CAN 'CHALLENGING THOUGHTS' HELP DEPRESSED MOODS?

Challenging unhelpful thinking and beliefs can be useful in lessening moods and chronic pain. It is not simply 'positive thinking'. It is about noticing thoughts that do not help in the present situation. They lead to unpleasant feelings of more depression and less pleasure. On the next page is a Challenging Thoughts Worksheet. This shows how new responses to a situation can improve the way you feel and think about it. Use this Challenging Thoughts Worksheet to spot and challenge thoughts that lead to unpleasant emotions or mood changes. Use a rating scale to check if challenging your thoughts led to an improvement in mood.

ACTION 3: HOW TO USE THE CHALLENGING THOUGHTS WORKSHEET

STEP A ('SOMETHING HAPPENS')

Write down in your notebook what happened, who was there and what you noticed.

Sometimes unpleasant feelings are more easily noticed than thoughts.

So you may need to use **Step C ('I feel and do something')** first, then go back to **Step A**.

STEP B ('I TELL MYSELF')

Record what your thoughts or beliefs were, and what you said to yourself.

Then check out your unhelpful thoughts, using the unhelpful thoughts list on p. 200.

STEP C ('I FEEL AND DO SOMETHING')

Record how you felt and what you did. Rate feelings (0–10)

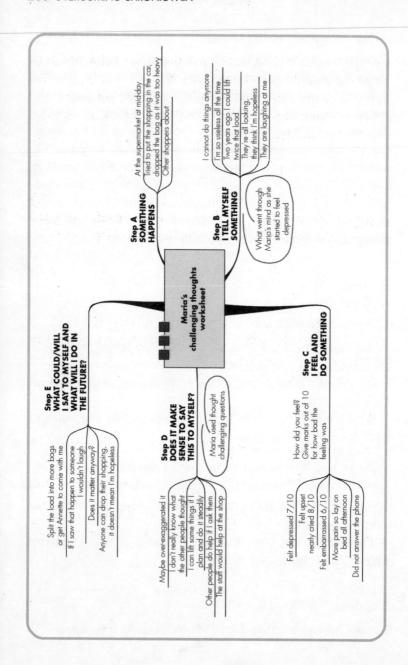

Maria's challenging thoughts worksheet

Step A SOMETHING HAPPENS
- At the supermarket at mid-day
- Tried to put the shopping in the car, dropped the bag as it was too heavy
- Other shoppers about

Step B I TELL MYSELF SOMETHING
- I cannot do things anymore
- I'm so useless all the time
- Two years ago I could lift twice that load
- They're all looking, they think I'm hopeless
- They are laughing at me

What went through Maria's mind as she started to feel depressed

Step C I FEEL AND DO SOMETHING
- How did you feel?
- Give marks out of 10 for how bad the feeling was
- Felt depressed 7/10
- Felt upset nearly cried 8/10
- Felt embarrassed 6/10
- More pain so lay on bed all afternoon
- Did not answer the phone

Step D DOES IT MAKE SENSE TO SAY THIS TO MYSELF?

Maria used thought challenging questions

- Maybe over-exaggerated it
- I don't really know what the other people thought
- I can lift some things if I plan and do it steadily
- Other people do help if I ask them
- The staff would help at the shop

Step E WHAT COULD/WILL I SAY TO MYSELF AND WHAT WILL I DO IN THE FUTURE?
- Split the load into more bags or get Annette to come with me
- If I saw that happen to someone I wouldn't laugh
- Does it matter anyway?
- Anyone can drop their shopping, it doesn't mean I'm hopeless

STEP D ('I ASK SOME USEFUL, REALISTIC QUESTIONS')

Use the 'Thought challenging questions' (see below) to challenge the thoughts you had in **Step B**.

Try to imagine different ways of seeing the situation.

See whether this changes your thoughts in a realistic, helpful way in **Step E**.

STEP E ('WHAT WILL I SAY TO MYSELF AND WHAT WILL I DO IN FUTURE?')

Record what you could or will say to yourself, using the results of the thought challenge in **Step D** to help you.

THOUGHT CHALLENGING QUESTIONS FOR STEP D

Step D – Ask myself:

What is the evidence for and against this thought?

If my best friend were in this situation, what would I say to him or her?

Am I confusing thoughts with fact?

Am I:

jumping to conclusions?

'mind reading'?

thinking in 'all or nothing' terms?

using words which are extreme or exaggerated (like 'always', 'never', 'mustn't', 'should', 'forever', 'can't' and 'every single time' . . .)

Use the 'Unhelpful thinking style list' on p. 202 to help you with this step.

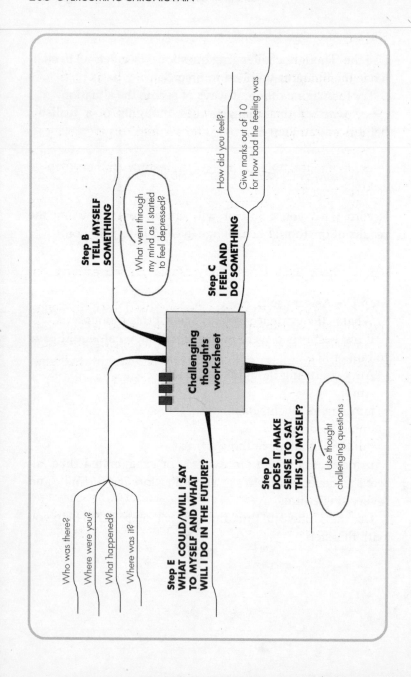

Step B
I TELL MYSELF SOMETHING

What went through my mind as I started to feel depressed?

Challenging thoughts worksheet

Step C
I FEEL AND DO SOMETHING

How did you feel?

Give marks out of 10 for how bad the feeling was

Step E
WHAT COULD/WILL I SAY TO MYSELF AND WHAT WILL I DO IN THE FUTURE?

Who was there?

Where were you?

What happened?

Where was it?

Step D
DOES IT MAKE SENSE TO SAY THIS TO MYSELF?

Use thought challenging questions

Am I:

- condemning myself as a person on the basis of this event?
- expecting myself to be perfect?
- concentrating on my weaknesses and forgetting my strengths?
- making judgements based on feelings rather than facts?
- focusing on factors that are irrelevant?
- paying attention to the negative side of things?

Finally, check what effect your realistic responses have on your mood level.

Note: Feedback from people who have used these Challenging Thoughts Worksheets suggests that it's worth trying them on at least three occasions when you are feeling depressed. It is really helpful to use the sheets until the thought challenge method becomes easy to do and a regular part of your life.

OTHER WAYS TO MANAGE DEPRESSION

Tick those ways you might try:

- ❑ Shifting attention and practising mindfulness (see Chapter 15).
- ❑ Increasing pleasurable activities. Rewarding yourself is a very useful way to help lessen depression. Try and do one pleasurable activity each day and then reward yourself for the effort (see Chapter 7).
- ❑ Changing unhelpful behaviors. Doing things that give you a sense of satisfaction or enjoyment. Plan activities day by day (see Chapters 6 and 8). Leave out or change unhelpful ones, like getting up late in the day.
- ❑ Becoming more physically active (see Chapter 9).

Using anti-depressants

Anti-depressants can be very useful in managing depression. These medicines can help change negative thinking and lift your mood. They take around two to four weeks to have any effect. You can reduce and then stop them at any time without serious lasting dependence symptoms. Talk to your doctor about ways to manage depression using medications and any concerns that you have about using them.

The most important thing is to take them every day for at least four to six months to help improve depressed moods. Depression can return if you stop and start anti-depressants, or if you do not take them for at least four months.

You can discuss the use of anti-depressants and length of drug treatment with your doctor, pain specialist or pharmacist (and see Useful Information at the back of this book for a list of self-help books on managing or overcoming depression, including the use of medication).

PART I SUMMARY

- Mood changes are very common in chronic pain. Understanding which moods can affect you is a helpful important step towards change.
- Depression is a very common experience in chronic pain. The person-centred model shows its effects and helps focus on what can be changed for the better.
- Understanding unhelpful thinking and challenging it, using thought challenge questions, can help lessen depressed moods. It may improve enjoyment, despite the pain.
- Using the chapters on rewards, getting fitter and being more active and acceptance will also help lessen depression.
- Your healthcare practitioner can help and anti-depressants can be useful to lessen depression and reduce relapse.

PART 2: MANAGING ANXIETY

This section aims to help you understand:

- What anxiety is
- What the effects of anxiety are
- How to manage anxiety by dealing with unhelpful thinking
- How to overcome avoidance
- How to change unhelpful behaviors

What is anxiety?

Anxiety can range from feeling a bit uneasy or nervous to having a continuing sense of dread. Sometimes anxiety can become so bad that the person feels panicky and frightened. We all feel anxious at certain times and this is normal. A certain level of anxiety can help us to perform at our best, whether in sport or giving a speech at a wedding or at a job interview. Anxiety is a problem when it is more severe than you would expect in the situation and when it affects your life. For example:

If you are often anxious

- When there seems to be no good reason for it
- If there is a lot of anxiety

What are the effects of anxiety?

Anxiety affects you in three main ways:

1 **Body symptoms and many different sensations**

Sweating, feeling shaky, pounding heart, choking feeling, dry mouth and dizziness are some of the many body sensations you may experience when you become anxious or worried.

2 **Unhelpful thinking and beliefs**

These lead to worrying, negative thoughts like 'What if . . .' or making negative predictions. Sometimes frightening images or pictures can occur, which in turn can make you feel anxious or frightened.

3 **Behaviors or actions**

Anxiety can either lead you to avoid doing certain activities or lead you to do things to keep yourself feeling safe in order to lessen anxiety.

The person-centred model of Jim (opposite) shows how anxiety can affect a person and their pain. It shows examples of the different stresses in a life situation that can cause anxiety or worry. It also shows the links between pain and feeling anxious or worried.

Jim still has shingles pain and no longer works as a teacher. He is anxious about his pain as, when he reaches into cupboards, he has bad shooting pains. He finds he is worrying about:

- *Ann's new swollen leg symptoms.*
- *If he can manage the garden on bad pain days.*
- *His memory, as he seems very forgetful some days. Even his daughter has noticed this problem in the last month.*
- *Going out into busy crowded places in case someone bumps into the left side of his chest and makes his pain worse.*

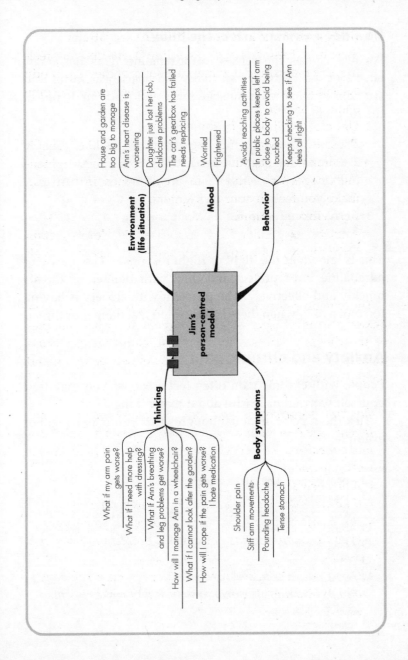

Environment (life situation)
- House and garden are too big to manage
- Ann's heart disease is worsening
- Daughter just lost her job, childcare problems
- The car's gearbox has failed needs replacing

Mood
- Worried
- Frightened

Behavior
- Avoids reaching activities
- In public places keeps left arm close to body to avoid being touched
- Keeps checking to see if Ann feels all right

Jim's person-centred model

Thinking
- What if my arm pain gets worse?
- What if I need more help with dressing?
- What if Ann's breathing and leg problems get worse?
- How will I manage Ann in a wheelchair?
- What if I cannot look after the garden?
- How will I cope if the pain gets worse?
- I hate medication

Body symptoms
- Shoulder pain
- Stiff arm movements
- Pounding headache
- Tense stomach

How does anxiety affect the body?

Anxiety causes the release of adrenaline. This has many effects in the body. It can make the heart beat faster and stronger or make your muscles tense and ready to do one of the following:

- Freeze on the spot, motionless
- Run as fast as possible, fleeing from the threat or danger
- Fight strongly against the danger or threat

This is known as the 'fight or flight response'. The release of adrenaline is to protect and deal with danger or threats quickly and effectively. The problem with anxiety is having too much of it, when there is little or no real danger or threat.

Anxiety and chronic pain

People with chronic pain often feel anxious. You may find yourself worried or fearful about many things.

Tick the type of anxious thoughts that you may have. For example:

- ❑ About the pain itself and its intensity
- ❑ About the causes of the pain
- ❑ About body symptoms, such as numbness or sleep problems
- ❑ About body movements or positions that increase the pain severely
- ❑ About staying at work or getting back to work or study
- ❑ About what other people might believe or think about you
- ❑ About whether people will reject you
- ❑ About what might happen if you become disabled and dependent on other people, possibly in a wheelchair
- ❑ Other fears?

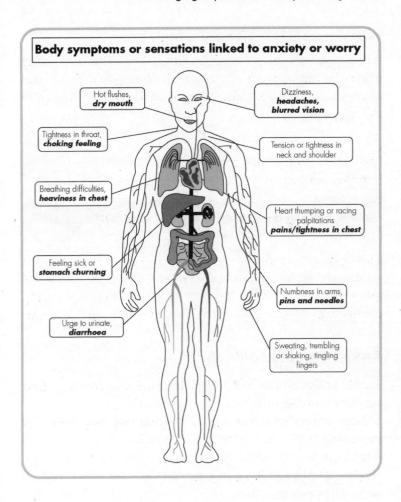

Body symptoms or sensations linked to anxiety or worry

Hot flushes, *dry mouth*

Dizziness, *headaches, blurred vision*

Tightness in throat, *choking feeling*

Tension or tightness in neck and shoulder

Breathing difficulties, *heaviness in chest*

Heart thumping or racing palpitations *pains/tightness in chest*

Feeling sick or *stomach churning*

Numbness in arms, *pins and needles*

Urge to urinate, *diarrhoea*

Sweating, trembling or shaking, tingling fingers

Write down any fears or concerns you may have in your notebook.

Managing anxiety by dealing with unhelpful thinking

When you become worried, anxious, scared or frightened, your thinking is likely to change in three ways. You may:

- Over-estimate the danger, the seriousness of the threat, or how vulnerable you are.
- Under-estimate your own ability to cope.
- Under-estimate your own resources or the 'rescue factors' in the situation.

Here is an example of how this type of unhelpful thinking works.

TABLE 14.3: UNHELPFUL THINKING

Situation	Unhelpful thoughts/ negative predictions	Feeling/ mood	Body sensations
You have to pick something up off the floor and you move awkwardly. You feel something pull painfully in your back.	This means the pain is going to be dreadful for the next few days. I'll never be able to manage to go to the shops for food and newspaper. I'll be stuck here – no one will be able to help.	Very worried.	Tight stomach, tense neck muscles, dry mouth.

This example shows a series of thoughts, or predictions, that increase anxiety. You strongly believe the predictions will happen, which is why you feel so anxious. This makes you feel more tight and tense in your muscles and joints. This, in itself, increases the pain.

WHAT ACTUALLY HAPPENED?

There was a mild increase in pain. The medication reduced it because it was an acute strain pain. The weather was sunny. You were in the garden and your neighbour saw you. She was going to the shops and offered you a lift in the car. You used distraction by working in the garden (**using your**

own resources). The lift from the neighbour was an example of a '**rescue factor**'.

So the predictions *were* inaccurate and this was an example of unhelpful thinking.

To manage this type of thinking, it helps to try the following actions:

- Identify unhelpful thoughts.
- Challenge unhelpful thinking using a worksheet and 'thought challenge' questions.
- Use helpful coping self-talk.

ACTION 1: IDENTIFY UNHELPFUL THOUGHTS

Think about the last time your mood changed to being anxious. Recall what went through your mind at the time. Then tick the style of unhelpful thoughts that you noticed:

- **All or nothing**
  Seeing things as either black or white. If something is not perfect, then it must be disastrous, yet life is not that clear-cut. It has many shades of grey.
- **Over-generalization**
  After one unfortunate event, assuming this will happen again, every time. There is no reason for seeing one instance as proving a rule for all events for always.
- **Mental filter**
  Picking out a negative or worrying detail and dwelling on it exclusively, so seeing the whole situation as bad. This will certainly make you feel worried and

you will no doubt be missing out on some positive sides of a situation.

- **Disqualifying the positive**

  Anxious people have a strong tendency to say that positive experiences don't count for some reason. You may say a successful event was a 'fluke'. You don't let yourself take pleasure from positive or pleasant events.

- **Jumping to conclusions**

  Assuming the worst when there is no real reason to think this way.

- **Catastrophic thinking**

  Exaggerating the importance of your own imperfections or errors or fears, e.g. 'I made a mistake – how awful – I can never show my face here again.'

- **Emotional reasoning**

  Believing, because you feel so afraid, that there really must be some danger. Sometimes things or situations feel so dreadful, you believe they really are in a mess. However, these anxious feelings are usually not realistic.

- **'Should' thinking**

  For instance, thinking you 'should' be able to stay calm all the time, or you 'must' never get angry. Such rigid thoughts are unreasonable, demanding and cause excessive pressure and, often, guilt feelings.

- **Labelling and mis-labelling**

  Labelling yourself 'a useless person' on the basis of a mistake you made. So your idea of yourself is because of something you have done? It makes as much sense as calling yourself an 'electrician' because you can change a plug!

- **Personalization**
  Assuming that when something goes badly, it was entirely your fault. Personalization usually causes guilt. It leads you to assume responsibility for events that are almost certainly due to many factors, *not* just you and your actions.

ACTION 2: CHALLENGE UNHELPFUL THOUGHTS

When you experience unpleasant anxious moods or emotions, notice what you are thinking.

Ask yourself: 'What went through my mind as I started to feel worried or scared?'

Moods can be affected by what you are thinking, and what you believe, about a situation. This is how Jim's thoughts and beliefs helped to make him feel very anxious.

JIM'S SITUATION	
Where?	At home, in the kitchen
When?	Wednesday afternoon, 13.30 p.m.
Who with?	Neighbour
What doing?	Sitting talking about the garden

Thoughts (What went through Jim's mind as he started to feel anxious?)

'What if I can't get out to cut the grass and tidy the flower beds? I am so useless. I used to be able to do all the tasks around the house. Everybody will criticize the state of the garden.'

Moods (emotions)

I feel so worried (7/10)

Body sensations

Felt tense in neck and back muscles, felt more pain

So Jim's **thought challenge**, using the thought challenge questions on p. 224, looked like this:

Does it make sense to tell myself that I am useless?

Do other people really criticize me because of the state of my garden when I am so limited by severe pain and stiffness?

Are these unhelpful predictions?

Jim's possible **realistic, balanced responses** were:

I have tried to get going this morning, the pain is very bad. That doesn't mean the garden will be in a state just because I am having a difficult day.
I am disappointed not to go out but it does not mean it is terrible.
I don't need to keep it neat and tidy. It doesn't reflect on me as a person. I can fail to do things some days without being 'a failure'.
In future, when I have that thought, I will tell myself I can only do my best at the time.

These realistic responses are likely to lift Jim's mood making him feel more cheerful and less worried.

So challenging unhelpful thoughts and beliefs can help lessen anxiety and chronic pain. Note: It is balanced, realistic thinking, not simply 'positive thinking'.

HOW TO USE A CHALLENGING THOUGHTS WORKSHEET

It can take some practise to notice when worried or upsetting thoughts are going through your mind, though sometimes they are all too obvious. Occasionally, anxious feelings are more easily noticed than thoughts. In this case, you can use the middle **Step C** ('I feel and do something') first. Use **Step**

JIM'S WORKSHEET

	Questions to ask yourself:	Jim's response
Step A Something happens	Who was there? Where were you? What happened? When was it?	Alone, in the house, cleaning the bedrooms stairs. Pain is really bad. Can't lift the vacuum cleaner up the stairs.
Step B I tell myself something	What were you thinking? What did you say to yourself?	I cannot do things at all. I am making a fool of myself. I'm so useless all the time. Ann and the family will think I'm hopeless. They will probably be laughing at me. I'll never cope with doing things around the house and garden.
Step C I feel and do something	How did you feel? Rate out of ten (10) how bad the feeling was? What happened afterwards? What was the consequence or result?	Felt very anxious (8/10). Felt embarrassed (6/10). Felt low (6/10). Tried to lift the vacuum cleaner up each stair and got stuck. Spent all afternoon weeding to get some jobs done and ease the pain.

| Step D Challenge the thought | Are my feelings reasonable? Are any of my thoughts unhelpful? Use the thought challenging questions list (see p. 224). | Maybe I magnified it. I don't really know what the family will think. I'm not useless all the time, as I can do some things around the house if I plan and do it steadily. Other people do help if I ask them. The family would help, if I asked them. |
| Step E Alternative, balanced realistic, responses | What could or will I say to myself in future? What will you say to yourself next time? Will you do anything different? | Next time – split the jobs up. Do it in parts, not all the rooms at once. Maybe on my bad days I could use a longer lead. If I saw that happen to someone, I wouldn't laugh. Does it matter that I was unable on one day to do tasks at home? I am not being hopeless. It just means the pain has limited my activities today. |

CHALLENGING THOUGHTS WORKSHEET

Step A Something happens	Questions to ask yourself: Who was there? Where were you? What happened? When was it? Describe the situation in which you had an unpleasant mood change	Your response
Step B I tell myself something	What were you thinking? What did you say to yourself?	
Step C I feel and do something	How did you feel? Rate out of ten (10) how bad the feeling was? What happened afterwards? What was the consequence or result?	
Step D Challenge the thought	Are my feelings reasonable? Are any of my thoughts unhelpful? Use the thought challenging questions list below.	
Step E Alternative, realistic, balanced responses	What could or will I say to myself in future? What will you say to yourself next time? Will you do anything different?	

C when you feel anxious. Then go back to **Step A** ('Something happens') and write down what happened, who was there and what you noticed at the time.

Now move to **Step B** and record what your thoughts were at the time, or what you said to yourself, or pictured in your mind.

Next, use **Step D** and **Step E** to start to 'challenge' your thoughts, and imagine different ways of seeing the situation. See if this affects your thoughts and lessens your feelings of anxiety by developing more realistic thoughts.

Use the sheet on page 222 to monitor and challenge thoughts that lead to unpleasant anxious moods. Use the 'Thought challenging questions' to help with **Step D** ('Does it make sense to say this to myself?').

Use this list of '**thought challenging questions**' to help you.

- Am I getting things out of proportion?
- If other people were in that situation what would I say to them?
- Am I confusing thoughts with fact? What happened the last time I was in this situation?
- Am I:

  (a) thinking in all or nothing terms?
  (b) jumping to conclusions?
  (c) using catastrophic thinking?
  (d) 'mind reading'?

- Are my thoughts predicting the future in an unhelpful way?
- Am I noticing only the negative side of things?
- Are my judgements made on the basis of feelings rather than facts?

Note: Feedback from people who have used these Challenging Thoughts Worksheets suggests that it's worth trying them on at least three occasions when you are feeling anxious. It is really helpful to use the sheets until the thought challenge method becomes easy to do and a regular part of your life.

Do persevere. It's normal to have setbacks or progress slowly. And remember to reward yourself regularly, especially for your efforts (see Chapter 7).

ACTION 3: USE HELPFUL COPING SELF-TALK

Tick those coping self-talk thoughts below you would use when anxious:

❑ Having anxiety is normal.
❑ It shows that I am alert.
❑ Anxiety is simply the effect of adrenaline on the body.
❑ These sensations are not dangerous or serious.
❑ I am having false alarms.
❑ I have made negative predictions before, which have not come true.
❑ I can watch my body sensations increase and decrease.
❑ Just accept it as anxiety passes and goes away.
❑ Others?

You might want to add some of your own and perhaps carry them with you on a card.

There are other useful ways to reduce anxiety and worry, which may help you manage pain and daily life better. For instance, relaxation, especially focusing on your breathing, can lessen the body sensations (see Chapter 12). Try to use your relaxation skills, as they can be a really effective way of reducing mild to moderate anxiety.

Overcoming avoidance

Avoidance means avoiding feared places, people, situations and activities, or even certain movements, which make you anxious or worried. This may seem to help reduce anxiety at the time. However, the disadvantage is that it keeps the symptoms of anxiety going for longer and more severely.

For example, a person with chronic pain may hold the unhelpful belief that he or she should not do or try certain movements because in the past they have caused more pain. This belief leads to the negative prediction that these movements might cause more pain now. It is true that avoiding bending movements *may* result in less pain more of the time. But it also means becoming stiff and tight in spinal muscles and joints. So, when moving to bend or trying to be active, the pain increases, thus proving the negative prediction.

An alternative, balanced, realistic response would be to gradually and steadily increase the feared movements or activities. This would actually stretch tight, tense, muscle groups, strengthen the joints, and improve stamina (see Chapter 9), helping the person to be:

- more active, despite the pain
- less anxious and physically tense
- in less pain

It is possible to overcome avoidance through a gradual process of graded exposure (or facing your fears, step by step) to people, places, situations or pain experiences that make you anxious:

- Choose a situation or activity where you become anxious or worried.
- Break this anxious situation or activity into small, achievable steps (see the goal ladder in Chapter 6, p. 107).
- Start with the step which is the least worrying or fearful.
- Think of breaking each step down further if necessary.
- Move up each step, staying with the anxiety sensations, perhaps using coping self-talk and relaxed breathing.

This is called a graded exposure to the feared activity or situation.

Note: Regular practice is the best way to make changes and become more confident. Doing it occasionally only helps a little, as you gain more confidence but it doesn't last. Remember to reward yourself for your efforts, repeatedly. Taking too many steps at one time can sometimes cause setbacks or flare-ups.

Here's an example:

Maria was very fearful of getting out of the bath. She had fallen badly on two occasions. Her unhelpful belief was a negative prediction: 'She would fall again and make her pain problems even worse.' Her shower was faulty. So she decided to tackle her fears about taking a bath.

MARIA'S GRADED EXPOSURE TASK

Maria works her way 'up the ladder' to achieve this goal, starting with the least frightening step.

TABLE 14.4: MARIA'S GRADED EXPOSURE TASK

Step number	Task/activity
Start: Least frightening situation:	Sitting on the side of the bath, fully dressed, holding on to the bath rail, feet on the floor.
1	Sitting on the side of the bath, feet on floor, not holding onto the rail at least twice per day.
2	Sitting on the bath side, dressed, not holding on to bath rail.
3	Sitting on bath side, swing one leg in. Practise exercise to help swing legs, especially the hips.
4	Sitting on bath side, swing both legs into bath.
5	Sitting on bath side, swing both legs and stand in bath dressed. Practise sitting-to-standing movements.
6	Sitting on side of bath, swing both legs and lower self into bath with stool in bath. Use grab rails to lift out.
7	Get into bath filled with water and take bath on stool.
8	Get into and out of dry bath without stool.
Most frightening situation:	Getting out of the bath, wet!!

Changing unhelpful behaviors

Some activities can increase or cause anxiety.

Tick any of these behaviors you have noticed in yourself and think about changing them steadily:

- ❑ Rushing round from one activity to another
- ❑ Drinking too much coffee/tea/cola
- ❑ Not allowing enough time to do particular tasks or activities
- ❑ Being in noisy, busy, places
- ❑ Being tired
- ❑ Being in pain
- ❑ Other activities, e.g. children always late

TEA/COFFEE/COLA – DRINKS WITH CAFFEINE

Maybe you could check out your caffeine intake and gradually make changes, if needed. How many cups or mugs of tea or coffee do you have in 24 hours? The sensible amount of tea or coffee per day is between two and three (cups or mugs). Caffeine stimulates the release of adrenaline so increases all your anxiety symptoms. It is important to have plenty of fluids, though, so you could try drinking more water. You could also have a go at herbal teas, fruit juice or decaffeinated coffee and tea.

PART II SUMMARY

- Anxiety is a normal feeling and can help you to perform at your best and deal with dangerous situations. But, if high levels of anxiety interfere with your life, and happen when there is no real danger, then anxiety is a problem.
- Identify what would be helpful to change, such as unhelpful thinking, unhelpful behaviors or avoidance of feared situations or movements.
- Reducing anxiety can help you manage your life and pain better. Trying out and practising changes gradually and regularly can be helpful to reduce anxiety or worry.

PART 3: MANAGING ANGER

This section aims to help you understand:

- How anger affects you and your pain
- How chronic pain and anger are linked
- How being angry can affect other people
- How to manage anger better

How anger affects you and your pain

Anger, frustration and irritation are common feelings when you have chronic pain. People have different ways of showing, or hiding, their anger. People with pain, who used to see themselves as 'easy-going', may find that they have a shorter fuse. Other people who have always had a temper may find that it flares up more easily and more frequently when they are in pain, especially when the pain is persistant.

However, anger is not a problem for everyone. Some people find that they are happy with the way they express anger. Others find that they do not get angry very easily. If you think that anger is unhelpful, especially in the way you manage your pain, this section may help. You may also find it useful to look back at the 'Challenging unhelpful thoughts' section in Part 1 ('Managing Depression') and Part 2 ('Managing Anxiety').

This section discusses how anger happens, and how it can be expressed in a 'healthy' way. It also offers advice on what to do if you think you need to deal with your anger differently.

WHAT FACTORS MAKE YOU ANGRY OR FRUSTRATED?

Several of these factors may affect your moods in other ways apart from anger and frustration.

Tick any factors that are important for you:

❑ Relationship issues or problems
❑ Work or home stresses
❑ Life events, e.g. job change, divorce, moving house, family illness
❑ Managing bills and budgeting; debt problems
❑ Unhelpful behaviors, e.g. drinking too much alcohol, using drugs like cannabis or heroin
❑ Changes in how you think, e.g. becoming extreme and negative ('all or nothing') in your thinking.
❑ Frustration about reduced levels of physical activity
❑ Not being able to keep up with demands placed on you, by yourself or by other people
❑ Losses in your life, e.g. job loss, loss of fitness and good health, loss of confidence, loss of plans for the future
❑ Lack of sleep
❑ Tiredness, low energy levels
❑ Side-effects of medicines

WHAT ARE THE EFFECTS OF ANGER ON YOURSELF AND YOUR PAIN?

The person-centred model in the mind map on p. 233 shows how anger can affect the five parts of a person.

Think back to the last time you felt angry. Then circle any parts of the map that match your own experience of the effects of anger.

Case history: Steve's angry moods

Steve was very irritable, especially on bad pain days when he was stuck in the house. He found himself thinking about how unfair it was that he could not cycle, go to work and had to take so many tablets. He had been much angrier ever since the accident, which was mainly the other driver's fault. He was not awarded compensation for the back pain. This was because of an earlier episode of back pain, two years before the accident. He thinks a lot about his problems, especially when the pain is bad.

Steve had realized several issues about his anger:

Nicole had told him for several months that he kept shouting at her and was more irritable.

He had yelled at his doctor's staff when there was a mix-up with his drug prescription.

On one occasion he had thrown his teacup against the lounge wall, as he could not find the remote control for the television.

He got very wound up if he was kept waiting when out at the shops or at health centres.

He was often worse after he had been drinking beer to ease the pain.

HOW DO YOUR THOUGHTS OR BELIEFS AFFECT THE WAY YOU EXPRESS ANGER?

When you have chronic pain, the beliefs you have about yourself, other people and your life may not make sense any more. The model on page 234 shows the effects of anger on Steve, especially his thoughts and behaviors.

How chronic pain and anger are linked

Chronic pain can lead people to be very easily irritated. It can mean that they think about themselves or other people in a negative and unhelpful way. Many people with pain have angry feelings at times. There is often a sense of unfairness.

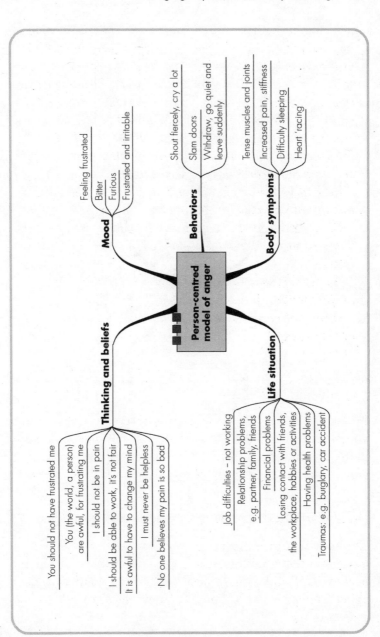

Person-centred model of anger

Mood
- Feeling frustrated
- Bitter
- Furious
- Frustrated and irritable

Behaviors
- Shout fiercely, cry a lot
- Slam doors
- Withdraw, go quiet and leave suddenly

Body symptoms
- Tense muscles and joints
- Increased pain, stiffness
- Difficulty sleeping
- Heart 'racing'

Thinking and beliefs
- You should not have frustrated me
- You (the world, a person) are awful, for frustrating me
- I should not be in pain
- I should be able to work, it's not fair
- It is awful to have to change my mind
- I must never be helpless
- No one believes my pain is so bad

Life situation
- Job difficulties – not working
- Relationship problems, e.g. partner, family, friends
- Financial problems
- Losing contact with friends, the workplace, hobbies or activities
- Having health problems
- Traumas: e.g. burglary, car accident

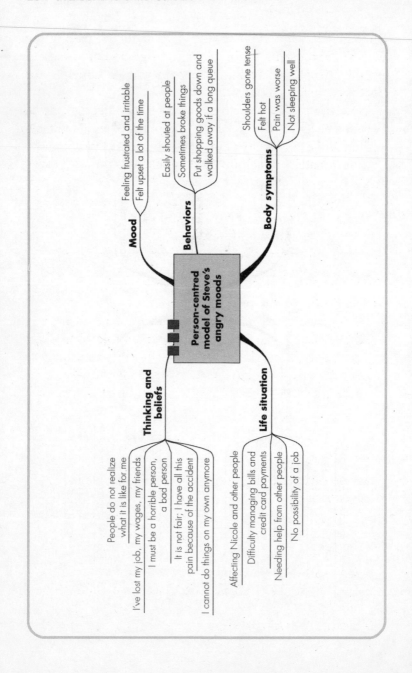

Mood
- Feeling frustrated and irritable
- Felt upset a lot of the time

Behaviors
- Easily shouted at people
- Sometimes broke things
- Put shopping goods down and walked away if a long queue

Body symptoms
- Shoulders gone tense
- Felt hot
- Pain was worse
- Not sleeping well

Person-centred model of Steve's angry moods

Thinking and beliefs
- People do not realize what it is like for me
- I've lost my job, my wages, my friends
- I must be a horrible person, a bad person
- It is not fair; I have all this pain because of the accident
- I cannot do things on my own anymore

Life situation
- Affecting Nicole and other people
- Difficulty managing bills and credit card payments
- Needing help from other people
- No possibility of a job

They may feel it is right to feel angry about the pain or the events that caused it. They can become angry because other people do not understand their pain and its unhelpful or distressing effects on them.

In Steve's case, the accident had not been his fault so he believed he had a right to be angry about it. Sometimes, even when there is no one to blame, life can still feel very unfair.

Unfortunately, unhelpful thinking like this can lead to:

- Increased tension in muscles and joints
- Paying attention to the pain
- Not noticing positive or enjoyable experiences
- Becoming tired

All these factors can, in turn, lead to more pain.

This does not mean that angry feelings and showing anger is 'bad'. It is more about *how* anger is expressed, or *how* intense it is and *how* it then affects you and your pain.

These are more helpful ways of dealing with anger, such as:

- Sharing feelings without blaming someone
- Asking for someone to change their behavior
- Trying to get fairness or justice in a respectful way
- Being realistic about the extent to which you have been treated unfairly
- Not seeing yourself as *totally* right or wrong
- Seeing the other person's point of view
- Getting things changed for the better, for yourself or others
- Deciding to stop plotting revenge

How being angry can affect other people

Being irritable can affect others you spend time with at home, at work or in other places. People may not understand your situation, especially people you don't know well. Relationships at home may become strained or tense. People in public places, such as shops or hospitals, may not understand the pain problem and the irritation and frustration you experience because of it.

Case history: Steve's anger affects his partner

Steve had always been close to his partner, Nicole. She had been happy to help more since Steve had had his accident. However, she became upset when he shouted at her. She said it was hard to 'know where I stand'. Sometimes Steve would shout and say she didn't 'understand how bad the pain is'. At other times, he would shout at her that she was 'treating him like a cripple'. She was beginning to find him hard to live with. They were both embarrassed when he lost his cool in public. Steve seemed to get even angrier when Nicole became upset, sometimes ending up in tears. He said he didn't mean to shout at her and really knew how much she cared. He was angry with himself for being angry.

Think about the people who are close to you, as well as people you meet in public places or at specific events. How does your anger affect all these people? Write your ideas in your notebook. It may help to think about the last few times you were angry.

Firstly, you can look at what happens when you start to feel angry, using the following questions to help you.

Something happens:
Where?
When?
Who with?
What am I/we doing?

Thoughts:
What went through my mind as I started to feel angry?

Moods (emotions):
How did I feel?

Body sensations:
What did I notice?

Behaviors:
What did I do or not do?

These observations will give you a better understanding of how anger affects you, especially your thoughts and behaviors. Then you can look at what makes a difference to the way you express anger and find out how you could handle anger better.

How to manage anger better

Here are some ideas about how to handle angry feelings differently. You can use these ideas to work out your own 'coping plan' for situations where you get angry or frustrated.

Steve used a 'coping plan' to make changes:

He talked his feelings over with Nicole when he was feeling calm and she helped him with his plan.

He practised the breathing exercise (see below) when he wasn't angry, so that he could remember to use it in difficult situations.

He found his bad temper was worse when the pain was severe. So he made a plan for coping with pain setbacks. This planning made him feel more confident about dealing with difficult times.

He practised saying to himself 'So what is the issue here?' to check his thinking.

He used the ideas below to help challenge unhelpful thoughts. The 'thinking of other explanations' was very helpful.

RESULT: Steve became less irritable as he began to handle events more calmly. He found the reception staff at the doctor's surgery quite friendly when he made appointments.

A 'coping plan' can be very helpful at times when you are becoming frustrated, or begin to feel insulted or attacked, and start to feel angry.

A coping plan

1: COPING WITH THE FIRST RUSH OF ADRENALINE (SOMETIMES CALLED AROUSAL)

The adrenaline rush of anger can lead to body sensations (like a thumping heart in the chest, getting hot and sweaty or shaking) that may increase the pain at the time.

Try self-talk as anger feelings rise, like:

- My muscles are getting tight, relax and slow things down.
- It's time to take a long, deep breath out first.
- My anger is a signal of what I need to do – problem-solving

2: IF ANGER CONTINUES TO RISE . . .

Don't respond immediately – pause.

Breathe OUT first, so as to feel yourself and your body relax. Focusing on your breathing can help you unwind. Taking a breath IN first can make you more tense, not less.

Make your OUT-breaths longer than your IN-breaths by counting to 4 for an out-breath and 3 for an in-breath for a least 2 minutes.

It is crucial to breathe slowly out first, **not** in first. This helps to reduce the adrenaline rush of anger that makes your heart race and makes you feel hot and tense. It also helps to reduce the tightness in your chest and other body sensations.

3: CHECKING YOUR THINKING

Useful questions to ask:

- What is making me angry?
- Have I listened properly?
- Have I got the facts here right?
- Have I got the whole story?

Think about what will happen afterwards if you react differently. What will the consequences be? Check out your thoughts again:

- Have I been clear about what I want?
- Have I jumped to conclusions and made a mistake?
- Are there any other reasons that could explain the situation?
- Is it worth getting angry about this at the moment?

Start to respond in non-aggressive ways, using methods that will control your anger. Try helpful self-talk, like:

- I am not going to let this wind me up.
- I can try my muscle-relaxing exercise.
- I can listen and try to understand the situation. I can ask questions to help us be clear about the problem.
- Maybe we will have time to think about it and talk later.
- I can cope with the pain. Getting angry will only make it worse. What's the point?

If you are dealing with conflict or being wound up by others, try saying to yourself:

- As long as I keep my cool, I'll be in control of the situation.
- I don't need to prove myself.
- STOP – there is no point in getting mad.
- Look for positives, and don't jump to conclusions.
- Let's take the issue point by point.
- It feels like they want me to get angry, but I will deal with it in helpful ways.

4: PREPARING FOR A SITUATION WHICH YOU KNOW CAN GET YOU ANGRY

Try saying some of these things to yourself:

- This situation has made me angry before, but I can deal with it.
- Remember to stick to the issues.
- Don't take it personally.
- There won't be any need for an argument.
- I know what to do. I have planned and rehearsed it.
- I will have some time out to help reduce angry feelings and to review and plan.
- Maybe the other person has chronic pain too!!!

5: AFTER THE EVENT

What you can say to yourself afterwards, when thinking about what happened?

Situation unsettled:

- Forget the aggravation, thinking about it gets me upset.
- Remember relaxation, it is better than anger and more pain.
- Don't take it personally.
- I can come up with a better way of dealing with the issue.

Situation settled:

- I handled that one pretty well.
- I could have got more upset but it was not worth it.
- My pride can get me into trouble but I'm doing better at this all the time.
- I got through that one without getting angry.

MAKING YOUR OWN COPING PLAN

When you make your own plan for dealing with situations that can make you angry, it will need to help you with two main areas:

Angry or frustrated thoughts and feelings

Body sensations, like getting flushed or hot, or if your heart pounds faster.

Ask yourself:

What can I do if I begin to feel insulted or attacked or frustrated, and start to feel angry?

Then write your plan in your notebook, starting:

'I can . . .'

Case history: Maria's plan for managing anger

Maria goes shopping with her daughter Janette, usually on a Wednesday. Sometimes Janette arrives late. This means that Maria has to rush her shopping. This makes her tense because she is worrying about when Janette will arrive. She knows if she rushes round the shops she gets more pain. It makes her irritable because she has to rely on her daughter. 'I wish I could manage it myself.'

Maria's plan

If feeling upset and cross

I can . . .

- Explain my concerns about the time and pain to Janette. She cannot read my mind.
- I can ask her if she could come another time.
- I can say to myself: 'Is it worth getting cross? At least I got out of the house.'
- Maybe it would help to make a plan if we are short of time.

If feeling body sensations caused by anger
I can . . .

- Try and watch out for the quick flash of temper when I am tired.
- Breathe slower and slow down my thinking and speech.
- Notice that I am getting tired. Let Janette know that we need to stop for a break.
- Postpone talking about important issues.

YOUR PLAN

In the same way, you can write down in your notebook what you plan to do, under the following headings. In each case, start with the phrase 'I can':

What can I do if I begin to feel insulted or attacked or frustrated and start to feel angry?

How can I cope with the body sensations I get when I am angry?

How can I prepare for a situation I know is likely to make me angry?

What can I say to myself when thinking later about what happened in the situation?

If it went well . . .

If it went less well . . .

PART III SUMMARY

- Anger can affect a person's feelings, thoughts, behaviors and body sensations.
- Anger can also affect chronic pain and it is important to express anger in a 'healthy' way.
- You can learn to respond in a helpful way to situations and deal with unhelpful thoughts, feelings and body sensations.
- Using coping plans can help you deal with situations that make you angry.

15

Acceptance

This chapter aims to help you understand:

- What acceptance is
- How acceptance can help you manage chronic pain
- What Attentional Control or Mindfulness is

Chronic pain can have a devastating effect on people's lives, often causing problems with relationships, finances and emotions. Other chapters in this book have looked at different ways of dealing with these problems, such as problem-solving (Chapter 10), relaxation (Chapter 12) and managing moods (Chapter 14). Acceptance is another vital factor in coping with problems resulting from chronic pain.

When real-life situations do not match expectations then emotional pain and distress can follow. There is a gap between what is or was expected, hoped for or the 'ideal' and what actually takes place or happens. And the bigger the gap, the greater the distress. Acceptance or coming to terms with your situation can bridge this gap and reduce the discomfort and distress.

To understand the gap that sometimes exists between reality and expectations, try the following exercise.

In your notebook, write two column headings:

The Real Me
and
The Ideal Me
Under 'The Real Me', write down your thoughts in answer to the questions:

- Who am I now?
- What is my life like?

Under 'The Ideal Me', write down your thoughts in answer to the questions:

- What did I expect to be?
- What do I think and feel things should be like?

What is acceptance?

When someone gives you a gift, you may feel excited or happy when you accept it. Trying to accept a situation or event that is negative or unwanted will probably cause you to react very differently. For example, trying to accept that a loved one has died may make someone feel sad, angry and fearful.

One definition of acceptance is: 'experiencing events fully, just as they are and not as they ought to be'. The mindfulness exercises later in this chapter (see p. 256) can help you learn how to 'experience events just as they are', without judging them as negative or positive.

Acceptance is not the same as 'giving up' or 'putting your head in the sand'. It is an ongoing process in which people with chronic pain can recognize that their real-life situation is difficult. It may not be what they would have chosen, but they can begin to look at themselves, others and the future in a different, more helpful way. Accepting what is happening can give you a sense of having some control over your circumstances and your future. It can also lead to a more hopeful, optimistic outlook.

MAKING SENSE OF LIFE

For centuries, human beings have searched for spiritual meaning and used different belief systems to explain or make sense of life. When things don't seem to 'make sense', it can take some effort to adjust to them in a helpful way.

For example, when in pain, bereaved or in crisis, people often ask: 'Why me?' or 'How did this happen?' In other words, they search for some 'meaning' in what has happened.

Case history: Steve

Steve found his back pain had got steadily worse over the months. Now, two years after the accident, he had given up work and spent a lot of time each day lying on his bed at home. He was sad and fed-up, and asked himself: 'What's the point in anything?' Steve had worked hard in his job. When he stopped work, he felt helpless and unable to change what had happened. Before the accident, he had expected to get promotion and he had been a good worker.

The pain meant that Steve:

- Could not work at his previous job, which he had enjoyed.
- Did not earn enough money to live the way he had expected to before.
- Had to agree with his partner, Nicole, that she would go out to work.
- Spent more time at home, often in bed.
- Had to accept that his plans for his future family would no longer be practical.
- Had low moods and felt distressed.

So there was a big gap between what he had planned and hoped for, and what was actually happening to him.

Now think about your own situation. Ask yourself:

- What does it mean to me to have chronic pain?
- How does the pain affect me, the people around me, and my future?

You may want to write down your answers in your notebook.

How can acceptance help you manage chronic pain?

Many people are familiar with the 'serenity prayer', often used by people with long-term health problems and difficult life situations:

> *. . . Grant me the serenity to*
> *Accept the things I cannot change,*
> *Courage to change the things I can,*
> *And the wisdom to know the difference.*

Acceptance is about finding ways of living with the things that you 'cannot change'.

This chapter is about getting used to what is left when you have done all that you can to change and manage better. It is also about grieving and coming to terms with the losses the pain has caused for you and others in your life, now and in the future. This can be one of the biggest challenges: accepting the idea that some pain may be there, however much you stick to your pain management plan.

Some people find that it helps to tell themselves: 'I cannot avoid pain but I do not have to suffer.' Changing your outlook on yourself and your future can be hard work and takes time. Spiritual beliefs can be helpful. For example, some spiritual teachings suggest that humans can experience 'inner healing' without necessarily being 'cured' of their illness or pain.

Having chronic pain can give you an opportunity to look again at what life means to you. It can be about finding new and *hopeful* meaning in your life situation. Events that may seem negative can also be seen as openings for growth, interest or new understanding.

HOW DID STEVE RESPOND TO THE IDEA OF ACCEPTANCE?

At first, Steve did not expect acceptance to help, because he believed it wouldn't change anything, especially the things he had lost in his life.

Steve had used other chapters to challenge some unhelpful thoughts, such as: 'I am useless' and 'It's not fair'. He had made some changes. For instance, he had spent some time with his partner, Nicole, looking at the household budget and working out how they could manage on a lower income. He had also managed to start pacing himself, and was getting a little more active.

However, he still had a lot of pain most days of the week. He realized that, however hard he tried, there was still going to be some pain. At times he was angry about it, but mostly sad.

He talked over the meaning of the pain with his best friend, Paul. His friend helped him to look at the possibilities that he had because he was at home. He came up with a list. (This took quite a long time!)

- I was 'there' for my mother when she had her heart attack.
- I can use a digital camera and I've got some great shots of the family.
- I could do some different training in electrical work and be better qualified.
- I am learning how to cook things on a low budget.
- I have met some lovely, caring people in the local self-help group.
- I have learned how to send emails.
- I have developed a website.
- I've been reading more. I never had time for it before and it helps with the forms and letters.
- I'm closer to my partner, Nicole. I've learned to talk about how I feel without blaming anyone.
- I've learned that I can be more patient and listen to other people more.

Steve was surprised at how many possibilities or benefits he came up with. He said it didn't make up for not being like he used to be. However he did find that he felt better and less frustrated when he thought about the benefits.

Now think about the opportunities that you have had, or could have, since having chronic pain. They can be small things, not just major ones. Talk it over with someone if it helps. This isn't about 'making up for the pain'. It is about seeing opportunities or chances, even though your life situation is not what you might have planned or expected.

Try to write down at least five opportunities in your notebook.

What is attentional control or mindfulness?

'Attentional control' or 'mindfulness' is about the kind of awareness that you bring to a situation. It means being in control of what you pay attention to, and for how long. It can be a helpful way of managing distress and many people have learned to manage their pain more successfully using it. Techniques like this are versions of meditation practices taken from Eastern spiritual traditions. The aim is to be in a 'state of mind' that is more helpful.

HOW CAN ATTENTIONAL CONTROL OR MINDFULNESS HELP?

Focusing attention on pain can open the pain gate (see Chapter 2, p. 45), which in turn will make you more aware of the pain. Becoming distressed by physical sensations can make the pain seem worse, and increase tension. Finding different ways of using your awareness, without necessarily becoming distressed, can be very helpful in managing chronic pain. It can also help to change the way that you experience the pain.

HOW DOES YOUR STATE OF MIND AFFECT YOU?

You may have already practised observing your thoughts in chapters 1 and 14 and so noticed then that the way you think has an effect on how you feel.

There are three 'states of mind' that people can bring to any situation. These are described below:

1. Reasonable (thinking reasonably)
In this state of mind, people:

- Think logically
- Pay attention to facts
- Plan your actions or behaviors
- Focus attention purposefully
- Take a 'cool' approach to problems

2. Emotional (thinking emotionally)
In this state of mind:

- Current emotional state controls behavior and thinking
- Thoughts are often extreme
- Logical, reasonable thinking is difficult
- Facts are distorted to fit feelings
- Intense feelings can motivate the person to continue with very hard tasks, or to make sacrifices for others

3. Wise (being mindful)
In this state of mind, people:

- Pay attention to unpleasant sensations without undue distress
- Avoid making value judgements (about themselves, others or the world)
- Become more aware of what they want to pay attention to
- Balance their emotions with reasonable thinking
- Act thoughtfully rather than on impulse
- Notice unpleasant feelings without the feelings being in control

Mindfulness aims to balance 'reasonable' and 'emotional' thinking, using a 'wise mind'.

Mindfulness skills

There are four main mindfulness skills: observing, being 'non-judgemental', focusing on one thing now and doing what works.

1. Observing
This means paying attention to events, emotions and behaviors:

- Without *necessarily* attempting to stop them if they are painful
- Without *necessarily* attempting to continue them if they are pleasurable

2. Being 'non-judgemental'
This means:

- Not judging something as either 'good' or 'bad'
- Looking at results of behaviors and events
- Describing the situation without judging
- Just looking at the facts

For example, you might notice that you have an increase in pain after an activity. However, it does not *necessarily* mean the outcome is 'bad'. It does not necessarily mean it is 'good' either!

3. Focusing on one thing now and being in the present
This means:

- Controlling your attention
- Not being distracted by memories of the past or worries about the future
- Not allowing negative moods or thoughts to get in the way

It is possible to learn to focus attention on one task or activity at a time.

4. Doing what works
This means:

- Focusing on achieving the goals you set yourself
- Realizing that what works well for one person or situation may not work for another
- Understanding that what used to work before, may not work now
- Realizing that doing what you 'ought' to do may not work for you in the present situation (e.g. being the sole breadwinner or making sure the ironing is done every day)
- Taking people as they are, rather than as you might think they 'should' be (including yourself)

Mindfulness exercises

Here are some exercises that you can do to experiment with attentional control or mindfulness.

AN INTRODUCTORY MINDFULNESS EXERCISE

- Give yourself a few minutes to sit quietly.
- Notice your breathing.
- Pay attention to your breath going in and coming out.
- Try to let your attention focus on the bottom of your in-breath.
- When you notice that your thoughts have wandered, bring your attention back to your breathing.
- Spend a few minutes bringing your attention back to the centre in this way.

This can lead to a state of feeling calm and secure.

AN OBSERVATION EXERCISE

- Be aware of your hand on a cool surface (e.g. a table or a glass of cold water). Be aware of your hand on a warm surface (e.g. your other hand).
- Pay attention to, and try to sense, your stomach and your shoulders.
- Stroke just above your upper lip. Stop stroking. Notice how long it takes before you cannot sense your upper lip any longer.
- 'Watch' the first two thoughts that come into your mind – just notice them.
- Imagine that your mind is a conveyor belt, and that thoughts and feelings are coming down the belt. Put each thought or feeling in a box near the belt.
- Count the thoughts or feelings as you have them.
- If you find yourself becoming distracted, observe that too! Observe yourself, as you notice that you are being distracted.

Note: It is usual to have to start and re-start several times when you practise 'stepping back' and observing in this way.

A 'DESCRIBING', 'NON-JUDGEMENTAL' EXERCISE

- Practise labelling thoughts in categories, such as 'thoughts about others' or 'thoughts about myself'.
- Use the 'conveyor belt' exercise described above. As the thoughts and feelings come down the conveyor belt, imagine sorting them into boxes, e.g. one box for thoughts, one box for sensations in your body, one for urges to do something, etc.

Make a point of practising **most often** the exercises that you find most difficult.

All these exercises will give you more control over what you focus your attention on. With a little practice, these skills can reduce the amount of distraction caused by pain. You will find it easier to deliberately pay attention to something else. This will help you 'accept the things you cannot change', while working on the things that you can change.

CHAPTER SUMMARY

- Acceptance can be helpful when other methods have been tried to overcome life situation difficulties.
- When losses have occurred, it is important to get used to what has happened, allow yourself to grieve for what has been lost, and learn how to cope with what is happening 'here and now'.
- Finding 'meaning' in what has happened, particularly noticing unexpected opportunities, can help.
- It is useful to go through a step-by-step problem-solving process. However, sometimes there is no 'perfect solution', and this is where acceptance can help.
- Your own values and view of the world can make it easier for you to cope with long-term difficulties. Some people find that spiritual practice or meditation can help.
- Mindfulness exercises are a useful practise. They can help you manage pain, while reducing suffering and distress.

16

Maintaining progress and managing setbacks

This chapter aims to help you understand:

- How to maintain progress
- What a setback is
- How to manage setbacks

How can you maintain progress?

There are many ways to maintain your progress and continue to build on your success and increase your confidence. You could:

- Vary your activities and exercises as they can soon become boring.
- Try fun and enjoyable ways to increase your activity level, like a game of crazy golf.
- Steadily increase your exercise routine.
- Set yourself short-term and long-term SMART goals (see Chapter 6).
- Reward yourself frequently and enjoy it (see Chapter 7)!

- Pace yourself (see Chapter 8).
- Prioritize, especially on bad days. Focus on what 'could' be done on that day or that week. Avoid the 'must' or 'should' type of thinking or I'll just do ... thinking.
- Keep a diary and record your progress.
- Learn a new skill (such as yoga or computer skills), or a new craft (like cross-stitch or painting) or take up a new hobby (like fishing, photography or model-making).
- Join a leisure group, such as a walking or line dancing group, or a gym, where qualified instructors can help design a programme to suit your needs.
- Tell others around you how they can help you (see Chapter 13). For instance, they could focus on your achievements or suggest rewards for your progress.
- Refresh your mind by reading this chapter regularly.
- Other? _____

In your notebook, write down your plan for maintaining progress, including at least three of the above points and/or your own ideas.

My plan for maintaining progress is:

1 _____
2 _____
3 _____

Obstacles to progress

There may be all sorts of obstacles and barriers that affect or even stop your progress.

Tick the factors that you think may affect your progress or stop you making changes in the future:

❑ Lack of time
❑ Lack of motivation or drive
❑ Too many interruptions
❑ Family issues
❑ Feeling better!
❑ Other factors, e.g. feeling very tired, being very angry

Now think about what might affect your progress now and write these difficulties in your notebook.

Work out some solutions and write them down too. It may help to look at the list of ideas on how to maintain progress (see above). You could also use Chapter 10 to help you with specific difficulties.

TIP

Try out the best solution overall!

What is a setback?

A setback may disrupt your daily routine or activities and can last for a few days or several weeks. It can often be due to a severe increase in pain. Or it can be linked to other factors, such as feeling very low, having a viral infection or a severe cold, family illness, a crisis with a child or elderly relative, having to do overtime at work, going on holiday, or worry over debts. A setback stops or limits many activities. It can make you feel down, disappointed or frustrated.

Think about any issues in your life that are likely to cause a setback, such as:

- Family
- Work
- Lack of time
- Going into hospital
- Moving house
- Travelling by car, bus or train
- Caring for an elderly or disabled family member
- Holiday
- Feeling low
- Other issues? _____

Depending on your own situation, some of these factors will be more likely or less likely to cause a setback. Mark the 'high risk' factors with (H) and the 'low risk' factors with (L).

Maria made the following list of issues that she felt were linked to her latest setback:

- My tooth pain and infection.
- Getting angry with my brother, John.
- Sleep problems, waking hourly.
- Having fallen out with the neighbours.
- Worrying about my sister Angela, who drinks too much alcohol, and who will look after her children.
- Not having enough money to pay the telephone bill.

TIP

Think about your last or current setback. In your notebook, write down what may have contributed to it.

Sadly, setbacks are inevitable. The good news is that what you do during a setback will make a real difference to:

- The impact it has on your day-to-day life
- The length of time it lasts
- How often you experience setbacks

How can you manage a setback?

Firstly, don't panic!! You don't need to stop everything. This is only a short-term problem. So reduce activities by between 40 and 50 per cent and increase relaxation skills. If you are forced to rest or spend time in bed, keep the time to a minimum. The longer you rest, the more difficult it is to get going again. You could also check your Positive Data Log (see Chapter 17) or list of goals (see Chapter 6) to help you focus on things you have achieved and things that are possible.

SOME WAYS TO MANAGE SETBACKS

Tick those that you will try:

- ❑ Keep doing your exercises but reduce them to half your normal level for a few days.
- ❑ Cut your sitting, standing and walking time limits in half.
- ❑ Use heat packs or ice packs.
- ❑ Increase your relaxation times.
- ❑ Use your pacing skills (see Chapter 8).
- ❑ Prioritize what could be done during the setback.
- ❑ Plan how you are gradually going to increase your exercises and activities (see Chapter 9).
- ❑ Set yourself SMART short-term goals (see Chapter 6).

❑ Keep a diary of what helped you to manage the setback this time. Inform family and friends about what they can do to help (see Chapter 13).

❑ Review (but don't dwell on) recent activities that may have caused the setback. What can you learn from this?

❑ If you need medication, then take it regularly, 'by the clock' (see Chapter 5). You may then be able to reduce gradually as the setback improves.

❑ Remember where you were before this setback. Focus on your achievements and not on the setback.

This is **Steve's** plan to manage a setback:

- Start my relaxation – deep breathing skills.
- Listen to my favourite rock music when I feel low.
- Do my three stretches, twice a day, just to the stretch sensation, not the pain.
- Check through my success list over the last four weeks.

In your notebook, write down the following questions:

What helped me in my current or last setback?

What will I do in my next setback?

Under each question heading, write a list of three or four points. When a setback comes, you need to know what to do and when. Working out a plan beforehand will help you act quickly.

CHAPTER SUMMARY

- Maintaining progress means pacing, planning and regularly rewarding yourself because you have kept going.
- Setbacks happen, and understanding what may trigger them will help.
- If you plan what you're going to do in case of a setback, it will be less likely to last a long time and interfere with daily life.
- Each setback offers a chance to learn better ways to manage pain. Remembering this will help you to stay confident and more active even in difficult times.

17

Looking to the future and managing work

This chapter aims to help you understand:

> * How new ways of life and new roles may be possible
> * How to use a Positive Data Log
> * How to think through work, study or retraining options
> * How to stay at, or return to, work successfully

How are new ways of life and new roles possible?

It is possible to change the impact of pain, steadily and slowly. You may need to start by thinking about what changes are possible in the short term or at this point in your life. It is also useful to keep a record of the changes you have made. This evidence of successes may help you realize that it is possible to return to, or stay at work, or develop new roles and skills. A Positive Data Log will enable you to build a record of your ability to cope or manage life despite the pain. Sometimes it is easy to overlook positive things that happen, so keeping a record can help to:

- Boost your confidence as changes happen
- Maintain your progress in getting active and reaching goals
- Remind you and others that change is possible, especially when you have a setback

How can you use a positive data log?

A Positive Data Log helps you to gather evidence that you are able to **manage or cope** with your life with your pain. You can start by filling the gap in the following sentence:

I am able to . . . . my life despite my pain.

Choose the word that seems right for you at present, in your situation. For example 'cope with', 'control' or 'manage'. Or you can use other words that seem best for you, such as, 'deal with' or 'accept' or even 'tolerate'. **Steve** chose 'cope with' for his log.

Step One: Write down the statement which best describes how you feel at present.

I am able to . . . . my life despite my pain.

For example, **Razia** wrote down:

'I am able to manage my pain and my life better.'

She used a log or diary. Each day she wrote down one piece of evidence of what she did, said, thought or felt that showed she was managing her life and her pain better.

Step Two: Write down a piece of evidence.

For example, Razia wrote:

'I managed to meet the children from school. They were so pleased to see me.'

It can be the same piece of evidence every day, e.g. 'I got up at 7 o'clock this morning, one hour earlier than normal.'

Or it can be different pieces of evidence, as in the following examples.

Steve's evidence in his log over three days was:

Monday: I walked for six minutes today, one minute longer than yesterday.

Tuesday: I prepared the dinner.

Wednesday: I did my exercises. I felt very calm after my relaxation.

Maria's evidence in her diary was:

Monday: I managed a bad pain day better by using my deep-breathing and stretch exercises.

Tuesday: I felt brighter so I put on my make-up and felt even better.

TIP

The Positive Data Log will help if you fill in one entry every day for at least four weeks. This is because there needs to be a lot of evidence to help you believe it!!

Step Three: Read through your log or diary each week, and see the evidence that you are coping or managing your life despite the pain.

Step Four: Ask yourself

'How much do I believe that "I am able to . . . . my life despite my pain."?'

For example, **Maria** rated her belief: 'I am able to manage my life despite the pain.'

Before she started this log, she rated her belief as 30%.

After she had used the log for four weeks, she rated it as 60%.

```
0%_____X_____X_____100%
No              Start           After four      Total
belief          of log          weeks
```

Mark an X on the line opposite when you start your Positive Data Log. Then mark another X after four weeks and see if there is an increase in your belief levels:

```
0%_____100%
No                                                  Total
belief                                              belief
```

TIP

It can help to be aware that sometimes the way we think can change the evidence and reduce its value (see Chapter 14 on 'Managing Depression, Anxiety and Anger').

These three things may happen to your thinking when you look at the evidence you have recorded. You may:

1 **Distort or dismiss** the evidence, by saying to yourself: 'Of course there is a change, that would happen anyhow.'
2 **Ignore** the evidence, by not even noticing that something positive has been said, done, thought or felt.
3 **Discount** the evidence, by saying: 'It's a fluke that I achieved my goal of walking to the shops this week.'

STARTING YOUR OWN POSITIVE DATA LOG

In your notebook, or diary, write a heading '**My Positive Data Log**'.

Begin with your statement:

I am able to . . . . my life despite my pain.

Choose the word that seems best for you, e.g. 'cope', 'control', 'manage', 'deal with' or ' accept'.

Then write your column headings as they are shown here:

Date   Evidence

Remember to keep your Positive Data Log for at least four weeks.

Thinking through work, training and other options

It has been found that people manage chronic or long-term conditions like heart disease better when they are doing something that they value. Doing something worthwhile can give you a sense of purpose, build confidence and boost your mood. Options might include paid work or volunteering, being a school governor, doing an evening class, or looking after grandchildren.

Improving skills in managing life despite the pain and being more confident can mean there is a real possibility of:

- Staying at work
- Returning to work
- Starting or continuing study or retraining
- Choosing other options, such as fostering or voluntary work
- Developing new roles or activities in life

Recent studies show that people with chronic pain have found many different ways to achieve their goal of staying at or returning to work. They have enjoyed themselves, had some fun, met new people and coped well with some difficult times on their route back to work or study.

It helps to think about both work and non-work activities, such as hobbies and voluntary activities. You can also consider how you would like to spend your days and nights.

It may help to revisit Chapter 1 ('Understanding the Impact of Pain'). This chapter looked at the changes you might wish to make in particular areas of your life, including work activities.

Start by thinking about your most important reasons for staying at or returning to work.

What are your main concerns about what this would involve for you at present?

Write your thoughts under two column headings in your notebook:

'**Most important reasons for staying at or returning to work**' and '**Main concerns**'.

How can you stay at work or return to work successfully?

If you have been on a pain management programme, or have worked through this book, then you will be used to learning and using new skills. Planning to stay at work or return to work can be made easier if you do it in stages.

It may be useful to begin by thinking about what would need to happen for you to return to or stay at work. You could use Chapter 10 to help you think of barriers that you would need to overcome.

> **TIP**
>
> Take these ideas one at a time, so you don't get overwhelmed or 'throw yourself in at the deep end'.

> **TIP**
>
> Try *not* to compare yourself with how you used to be before your pain, even though this can be a challenge!

Now think how it might be possible to stay at work in your current job. It may help to think through the advantages and possible disadvantages of returning to your current job. Write your thoughts under two column headings in your notebook:

'**Advantages**' and '**Disadvantages**'.

Once you have thought about the advantages and disadvantages, you will have some ideas about your next steps. Here are some suggestions.

WHAT MAY HELP YOU TO STAY AT WORK WITHOUT HAVING TO TAKE TOO MUCH TIME OFF?

You can apply what you have learned in other chapters of this book to the workplace. For example, skills like pacing and balancing activity and rest breaks can be useful (see Chapter 8). You might also need to break particular jobs down into steps as you would in other areas of your life. If the people in your workplace are not used to the kind of challenges you face, you might need to be more assertive and communicate your specific needs more clearly.

Workplaces in the UK are now required by law to provide for their employees if they have particular needs. This might apply in some situations if you have chronic pain. For example:

- Your employer might need to have your workstation adapted so that you can be more comfortable.
- There might need to be agreed break times so that you can stretch your body more often.
- You might need to have regular opportunities use relaxation skills.

HOW CAN YOU GET HELP TO ENABLE YOU TO STAY AT WORK?

There are various people who may be able to help. For example:

> - A talk with your manager or supervisor could help them to understand your needs.
> - A trade union representative may be able to work with you and your employer.
> - In larger organizations, there may be policies for helping people to stay at work, e.g. support for flexible working hours. You may need to talk to someone in the Personnel or Human Resources Department about this.
> - Occupational health services can help you get the right type of support or equipment or negotiate with workplace managers or staff.
> - Job support services, like Shaw Trust, can help you plan your needs and work with employers.
> - Contacting other people who have returned to work can give you useful information about what helps and who to talk to.

WHAT MAY HELP YOU RETURN TO YOUR CURRENT WORK AFTER BEING ON SICK LEAVE?

Often, when you are ready to start work, a gradual or 'phased' return is arranged. This means starting with a lower workload and slowly increasing your hours of work over several weeks.

Talk to your Personnel or Human Resources Department, or your immediate manager, to explain that you need to plan and pace your hours of work as you go back. Setting realistic and achievable targets will help you make a successful and consistent return. Planning in this way, and making the necessary changes to suit your needs in your workplace, can really make a difference to managing your working day.

There are often schemes available to help people who are employed but are off work due to ill-health. For example, there are some Employee Assistance schemes that are aimed at people who have been off work for a long time, sometimes months or years. More and more people are making a successful return to work this way – after cancer treatments, heart attacks and accidents, as well as pain problems.

WHAT MAY HELP YOU RETURN TO WORK WHEN YOU NEED TO FIND A DIFFERENT KIND OF WORK?

Some of the useful steps that may help you find a different kind of work include:

- Thinking about what might be possible (making a list of options).
- Thinking and sharing ideas or possible solutions with otherswho have returned to work after a long time not working.
- Asking yourself: 'How would I like my life to be if I was working?'
- Asking yourself: 'How would I like to feel if I was working?'
- Finding out what is available in the way of professional support or organizations to help.
- Making a list of all the activities, hobbies or skills you have used in the workplace or at home, or in life outside work and home.

Steve had wanted to go back to work but realized that working in electronics was no longer realistic. He quite liked driving and his younger sister begged him to teach her how to drive. He was delighted when she passed her driving test first time.

He asked around for ideas from friends and family about how to use his driving skills and came up with the following list of options or ideas:

- Check what is needed to drive, including insurance.
- Check out what courses there are that could use my driving skills in other ways.
- Check out regulations about driving public vehicles.
- Talk to contacts at the local bike shops and friends at the local garage.
- Check out local notice boards, and websites and biking- or driving-related magazines.
- Ask if the local hospice and hospital want volunteer drivers.
- Improve wing mirrors on the car because of back pain and stiffness.

By chance, some of Steve's biking mates wanted to have a night out and come back late. Steve suggested he could drive them there and back, as he did not drink because of his medication.

This worked out well. It helped increase Steve's confidence, as he realized that maybe he could do this as a job. He decided short trips would be best. So he made contact with the local hospice and signed up as a volunteer. He loved the work and really felt he was helping others. He went on to help out with the rotas for the drivers for the hospice. Slowly he realized that he could be dependable despite the pain. He risked applying for a part-time job at a car hire company, picking up and dropping off cars for customers. He got the job. He and Nicole celebrated with a meal out when he finished his first month of paid work. He felt able to start a repayment plan for his loans from his bank and his mother. Overall this goal took him nine months to achieve.

WHAT OR WHO WOULD HELP ME TO PREPARE FOR STARTING WORK?

If you are not working at the moment, there are a number of different options.

Tick the ones that you might try:

- ❑ Contact the JobCentrePlus advisers at your local Job Centre.
- ❑ The Disability Employment Adviser is based at the JobCentre and knows how to negotiate on behalf of people who have specific needs (for example, if you wish to try out a job placement or a course, before committing to it). These advisers are also experienced at agreeing special hours, or arranging for specific equipment for the workplace.
- ❑ Job Brokers, like the Shaw Trust, can be contacted through the JobCentrePlus. Job brokers have special experience of supporting people who have been off work for months or years. They are aware that people might need to take things steadily or have extra help. They give assistance with application forms, preparing for interviews and how to present yourself.
- ❑ Careers advisers are skilled in helping you to identify skills that you do not necessarily give yourself credit for. For example, you may be very talented at managing a limited budget. Planning activities, such as looking after children or cooking meals, also requires organizational skills. Many employers see determination in the face of difficulties as a positive asset.
- ❑ Start your own business. Some people decide to become self-employed so that they can work flexible hours or be based at home. Local business advice services are usually very helpful, with

courses and even grants available in some situations. You can talk over your ideas, and the strengths you have as well as the challenges.

❑ Local business advice, networking and courses from the Chamber of Commerce are often free.

Schemes do vary in different areas, so it's worth exploring the possibilities at job or employment centres, your local Citizens' Advice Bureau and local community resources or information centres. You do not always have to start with a definite job in mind. There are opportunities to try things out for several weeks or even months without losing your benefits.

WHAT ABOUT VOLUNTEERING AND COMMUNITY ACTIVITIES?

The first steps to returning to work can seem frightening – especially if you have not worked for some time or if you are unable to work in your previous role, like Steve or Maria. However, taking the first steps doesn't necessarily mean applying for a job straight away. Several of the schemes mentioned above support people in starting with some voluntary work or a course, without losing their benefits.

In most areas, there is a volunteer agency, where you can discuss various ideas about what you might like to do, and try things out before you make a commitment. Maybe you know someone who volunteers already? Or you might have a favourite local or national charity.

For example, **Maria** had always loved dancing, especially waltzes. She thought she could manage two hours of work, three days a week. She discovered that the over-fifties dance club at her local community centre needed help with after-noon teas. She then slowly increased her time, over four weeks, to four hours per day, three days a week. She was thrilled, and realized how important it was to pace her days. She made an entry in her Positive Data Log:

'I managed a whole week at work.'

This evidence helped her believe even more firmly: 'I am able to manage my life despite the pain. I think I could help out now, one morning a week, with Meals on Wheels as well.'

WHAT ABOUT COURSES AND COMMUNITY ACTIVITIES?

Going on a course can be an excellent way of starting to build your confidence and make new contacts, as well as increasing your skills. If you have been away from learning for a while, start with something you think will be fun and interesting. Many colleges do a broad range of courses, including day and evening classes, part-time and access courses, which suit different people. They often offer extra support for people with particular needs. If you need to change your type of work, retraining can also help you to find some new and really satisfying employment.

You might also find community activities going on in your local area, whether it is wildlife walks or classes on simple furniture repairs. Try looking for notices in your local library or local shops to see what is happening and start by just attending. You might want to offer to help out later. Another step on the way!

CHAPTER SUMMARY

- Keeping yourself at work, going back to work or finding other worthwhile activities can give you a sense of purpose.

- Using a Positive Data Log helps you to remember evidence of successes and keep a record of things that go well.

- When you begin to consider your role and what you want to do, you may want to look at work, either paid or unpaid, as well as courses, or voluntary and community work. There are many organizations and agencies that can help.

- Disability Employment Advisers and Occupational Health Departments, Human Resources Departments and your Union can all help with workplace issues.

- The JobCentre, job brokers, like Shaw Trust, and employment agencies can all be sources of support, advice and extra help, whether you already know what you want to do, or need help deciding where to start.

- Local colleges often provide a wide choice of different part-time and full-time courses, with extra support for students who need it. Doing a course could help you get into a new area of employment, gain self-confidence, feel a sense of purpose and enjoy meeting new people. Trying the local library or community resource centre might give you ideas.

- Volunteers are often welcome in a wide range of roles. Voluntary work can be satisfying in itself. It can also give you more confidence and experience to bring to an employer in the future.

Useful information

This section contains information sources and organizations. These can offer support and information about a range of chronic pain conditions and ways to manage them.

Professional organizations

British Association for Behavioral and Cognitive Psychotherapies
19 The Globe Centre St James' Square
Accrington
Lancashire BB5 ORE
Tel: 01254 875277
Fax: 01254 239114
Email: babcp@babcp.com
Website: www.babcp.com

British Psychological Society
St Andrews House
48 Princess Road East
Leicester LE1 7DR
Tel: 0116 254 9568
Fax: 0116 247 0787
Email: enquiry@bps.org.uk

Chartered Society of Physiotherapy
14 Bedford Row
London WC1R 4ED
Tel: 020 7306 6666
Fax: 020 7306 6611
Website:www.csp.org

Department of Health
Richmond House
79 Whitehall
London SW1A 2NL.
Website: www.dh.gov.uk

The Pain Relief Foundation
Clinical Sciences Centre
University Hospital Aintree
Lower Lane
Liverpool L9 7AL
Tel: 0151 529 5820
Website: www.painrelieffoundation.org.uk

The Pain Society
The Secretariat
The Pain Society
21 Portland Place
London W1B 1PY
Tel: 020 7631 8870
Website: www.britishpainsociety.org

Self-help groups and organizations

Action on Pain
20 Necton Road
Little Dunham
Norfolk PE32 2DN
Tel: 01760 725993
Helpline: 0845 603 1593
Email: info@action-on-pain.co.uk
www.action-on-pain.co.uk

Arachnoiditis Trust UK
Freepost
Head Office
PO Box 101
Ripon
North Yorkshire HG4 2ZR
Tel: 01765 605 668

Helpline: 0113 2880 121
Fax: 0870 135 6916
Email: information@arachnoiditistrust.org

Arthritis Care
18 Stephenson Way
London NW1 2HD
Helpline: 0808 800 4050
Website: www.arthritiscare.org.uk

Arthritis Research Campaign
Copeman House
St Mary's Court
St Mary's Gate
Chesterfield
Derbyshire S41 7TD
Tel: 0870 850 5000
Website: www.arc.org.uk

BackCare
16 Elmtree Road
Teddington
Middlesex TW11 8ST
Tel: 020 8977 5474
Website: www.backcare.org.uk

BBC
Website: www.bbc.co.uk/health/

Citizens Advice Bureau
Website: www.citizensadvice.org.uk

Cochrane Collaboration
Providing up-to-date information about the effects of healthcare inter-
ventions.
Website: www.cocohrane.org

Depression Alliance
35 Westminster Bridge Road
London SE1 7JB
Tel: 020 7633 0557
Website: www.depressionalliance.org

DIAL UK
St Catherine's
Tickhill Road
Doncaster DN4 8QN
Tel: 01302 310 123
Website: www.dialuk.org.uk

Fibromyalgia Association UK
PO Box 206
Stourbridge
West Midlands DY9 8YL
Helpline: 0870 220 1232
Website: www.fibromyalgiaassociationuk.org

Herpes Viruses Association
41 North Road
London N7 9DP
Tel: 020 7609 9061
Website: www.herpes.org.uk

JobCentrePlus
Website: www.jobcentreplus.gov.uk

ME (Myalgic Encephalopathy)
Action for ME
PO Box 1302
Wells
Somerset BA5 1YE
Tel: 01749 670 799
Website: www.afme.org.uk

Migraine Action Association
Unit 6
Oakley Hay Lodge Business Park
Great Folds Road
Great Oakley
Northants NN18 9AS
Tel: 01536 461 333
Website: www.migraine.org.uk

Mind
National Association for Mental Health
www.mind.org.uk

National Electronic Library for Health
Website: www.nelh.nhs.uk

National Endometriosis Society
50 Westminster Palace Gardens
Artillery Row
London SW1P 1RL
Helpline: 0808 808 2227
Website: www.endo.org.uk

National Osteoporosis Society
Manor Farm
Skinners Hill
Camerton
Bath BA2 0PJ
Helpline: 01761 471 771
Website: www.nos.org.uk

NHS Direct Online
Website: www.nhsdirect.nhs.uk

No Panic
93 Brands Farm Way
Telford
Shropshire TF3 2JQ
Free helpline: 0808 808 0545
Office tel: 01952 590005
Fax: 01952 270962
Email: ceo@nopanic.org.uk
Website: www.nopanic.org.uk

Pain Association of Scotland
Head Office
Cramond House
Cramond Glebe Rd
Edinburgh EH4 6NS
Tel: 0800 783 6059
Website: www.painassociation.com

Pain Concern
PO Box 13256
Haddington EH41 4YD
Tel: 01620 822572

Fax: 01620 829138
Email: painconcern@btinternet.com
Website: www.painconcern.org.uk

Reflex Sympathetic Dystrophy
RSD UK
323 Leymoor Road
Golcar
Huddersfield HD7 4QQ
Website: www.rsd-crps.co.uk

Relate
Herbert Gray College
Little Church Street
Rugby CV21 3AP
Website: www.relate.org.uk

RSI (Repetitive Strain Injury)
RSI Association
380–384 Harrow Road
London W9 2HU
Helpline: 0800 018 5012
Website: www.rsi.websitehostingservices.co.uk

Shaw Trust
Fox Talbot House
Greenways Business Park
Melmesbury Road
Chippenham
Wiltshire SN15 1BN
Tel: 01225 716300
Website: www.shaw-trust.org.uk

Spinal Injuries Association
76 St James' Lane
London N10 3DF
Tel: 020 8444 2121/0800 980 0501
Website: www.spinal.co.uk

Trigeminal Neuralgia Association UK
PO Box 413
Bromley
BR2 9XS

Tel: 020 8462 9122
Website: www.tna-uk.org.uk

Triumph Over Phobia
TOP UK
PO Box 344
Bristol BS34 8ZR
Tel: 0845 600 9601
Email: triumphoverphobia@blueyonder.co.uk
Website: www.triumphoverphobia.com

Books and publications

Coping Successfully with Pain, Neville Shone (Sheldon Press, London, 1992)
Coping Successfully with RSI, Maggie Black and Penny Gray (Sheldon Press, London)
Explain Pain, Lorimer Moseley and David Butler (NOI Press, 2003, www.noigroup.com)
Living With Back Pain, Helen Parker and Chris Main (Manchester University Press, Manchester, 1993)
Managing Pain Before It Manages You (2nd ed.), Margaret Caudill (Guilford Press, New York, 2002)
Manage Your Pain, Dr Michael Nicholas (Souvenir Press, London, 2003)
Mastering Pain, R. A. Sternbach (Ballantine Books, 1987)
Pain: The Science of Suffering, P. D. Wall (Weidenfield & Nicholson, London, 1999)
The Pain Relief Handbook, Chris Wells and Graham Nown (1993) (Optima, London, 1993)

Self-help books

Feeling Good – the New Mood Therapy, Dr David Burns (Avon Books, 1980)
Love is Never Enough: How Couples Can Overcome Misunderstandings, Resolve Conflicts, and Solve Relationship Problems through Cognitive Therapy, Aaron T. Beck (Harper Collins, New York, 1989)
Manage Your Mind, Gillian Butler and Tony Hope (Oxford Paperbacks, 1995)
Mind Over Mood, D. Greenberger and C. Padesky (Guilford Press, New York, 1995)

Overcoming Anxiety, Helen Kennerly (Constable & Robinson Ltd, London, 2007)

Overcoming Depression, Chris Williams (Arnold Publishers, London, 2001)

Overcoming Depression, Paul Gilbert (Constable & Robinson Ltd, London, 2007)

Overcoming Traumatic Stress, Claudia Herbert (Constable & Robinson Ltd, London, 1999)

The Illustrated Guide to Better Sex for People with Chronic Pain, R. Rothrock and Gabriella D'Amore

Contact Pain Concern (see p. 285) for booklet.

Tapes and CDs

Coping with Pain
Coping with Headaches and Migraine
Coping with Back Pain
Feeling Good (assertiveness and self-esteem)
Available as *Pain Management Packs* (3 different pack options) or individually
Produced by Talking Life, in conjunction with the Pain Relief Foundation, Walton Hospital, Liverpool.
Details from:
Talking Life
PO Box 1
Wirral CH47 7DD
Tel: 0151 632 0662
Website: www.talkinglife.co.uk
Single Cassette/CD: *Living with Chronic Pain*
Produced by Consultant Clinical Psychologist, Neil Berry.
Please send a postal order or cheque for £5.00, made payable to 'Pain CD', to:
PO Box 84
Blackburn BB2 7GH
Please indicate whether you require CD or cassette.

Useful videos

The *Pain Management Programme* video produced by Gloucester Pain Management Programme, Royal Gloucester Infirmary, Gloucester GL1 3NN.

Wordlist

Acute pain
: A predictable, time-limited response to injury, following chemical, thermal (heat) or mechanical tissue damage.

Anaemia
: Reduced number of red blood cells in the blood, which may lead to tiredness.

Ankylosing spondylitis
: A chronic inflammatory disease mainly affecting the spine, resulting in stiffness and loss of movement.

Barriers/blocks
: Factors that may get in the way and stop to progressyou achieving what you set out to do, e.g. a heavy cold, a row with the boss, a windy day.

Bone scan
: Investigation to test abnormal activity inside bones, which may come from tumours or infection.

Chronic pain
: Pain that has been present for three months orlonger. Chronic pain is long-term pain that seems to continue after the normal accepted time of healing for most tissues.

Congenital
: Disorder that has existed in the body since birth.

CT scan
: This type of scan assesses health and disease in body organs like the kidney and structures like the spinal cord and discs, as well as bones and muscles. The radiation from a CT scan is equivalent to 500 chest x-rays.

De-conditioned
: Poor level of fitness in muscles and joints due to reduced level of physical activity.

Fibromyalgia
: A widespread chronic pain condition of unknown cause, characterized by tender areas in muscles and poor sleep.

Flexibility	Ability to feel more mobile and less stiff, e.g. so you can put your socks on in the morning.
Goal setting	A skill that helps focus your efforts on achieving milestones.
Goal ladder	The gradual stages that you may achieve, over a time period, in order to reach your ultimate goal, e.g. to walk the dog or return to work.
MRI scan	This type of scan assesses healthy and diseased tissues in the body. It is used to assess all parts of the body, including muscles, joints and spinal discs.
Neuropathic	Name given to disorders of nerves caused by nerve injury, inflammation or degeneration.
Osteomyelitis	Infection usually caused by bacteria in the bone tissue.
Osteoporosis	Loss of structure and density of bones, especially in the spine, wrist and hip.
Pacing	A skill to help you monitor and plan your activity to make sure that you are not doing too much or too little.
PALS	Patient Advocacy Liaison Service, a service provided in NHS hospitals to help patients find out about and use the services available for their care.
Peripheral neuropathy	Disorder affecting the nerves, causing distorted sensations like burning as well as pain. It happens mainly in arms and legs.
Physical activity	Doing things that help you to become fitter, stronger and more mobile.
Radiographers	Staff who carry out x–rays, CT and MRI scan tests.
Radiologists	Specialist doctors who assess, interpret and make reports on x–rays and scans.
Rheumatoid arthritis	A disease affecting joints, causing pain and swollen, sometimes hot, joints. Rarely causes bone changes and deformity of the joints.
Sensory	A term used by doctors to describe a range of body feelings that nerves detect, such as cold, heat, pain, touch, vibration, position of joints.

Setback	An event, illness or increase in pain that disrupts your daily routine for a short time.
Spondylosis	A normal ageing process in the small joints of the spine that sometimes causes pain and stiffness.
Stamina	Ability to keep going for longer, e.g. vacuuming, walking.
Strength	Ability to work hard and do activities that require extra effort, e.g. climbing a flight of stairs.

Appendix

MY GOAL LADDER

My goal is

Time:

Week number	Activities to help me achieve my goal	Things that help my progress	Things that block my progress

Here is a spare Daily Activity Plan for your own use.

DAILY ACTIVITY PLAN

Time period	Activity
7.00 a.m.	
7.30 a.m.	
8.30 a.m.	
9.30 a.m.	
10.30 a.m.	
11.30 a.m.	
12.30 p.m.	
2.00 p.m.	
3.00 p.m.	
4.00 p.m.	
5.00 p.m.	
6.00 p.m.	
7.00 p.m.	
8.00 p.m.	
9.00 p.m.	
10.00 p.m.	
11.00 p.m.	
12.00 a.m.–7.00 a.m.	

SPARE MEDICINES USE DIARY

Situation	Pain level 0–10	Type of medication and how many taken
Who am I with? What am I doing? When? Where? (place) What mood at the time?		
Who am I with? What am I doing? When? Where? (place) What mood at the time?		
Who am I with? What am I doing? When? Where? (place) What mood at the time?		
Who am I with? What am I doing? When? Where? (place) What mood at the time?		
Who am I with? What am I doing? When? Where? (place) What mood at the time?		
Who am I with? What am I doing? When? Where? (place) What mood at the time?		

Suggested sexual positions for chronic pain sufferers

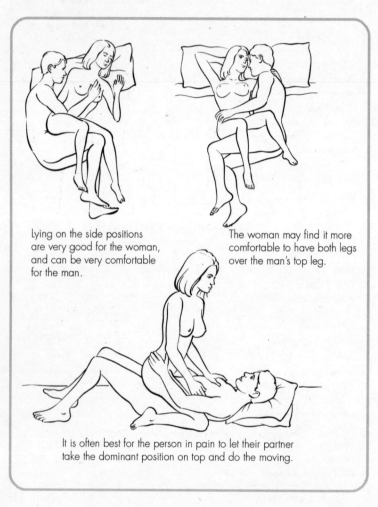

Lying on the side positions are very good for the woman, and can be very comfortable for the man.

The woman may find it more comfortable to have both legs over the man's top leg.

It is often best for the person in pain to let their partner take the dominant position on top and do the moving.

Suggested stretches

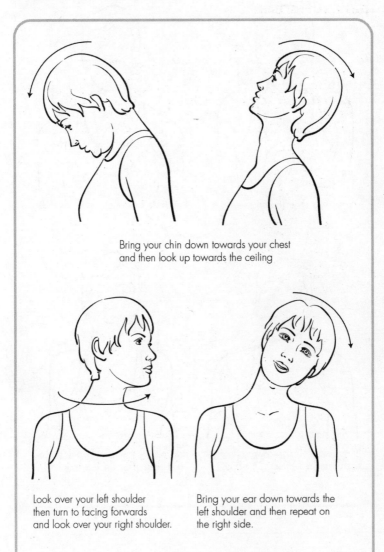

Bring your chin down towards your chest and then look up towards the ceiling

Look over your left shoulder then turn to facing forwards and look over your right shoulder.

Bring your ear down towards the left shoulder and then repeat on the right side.

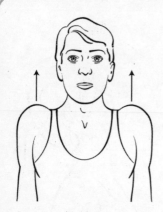

Bring your shoulders up towards your ears.

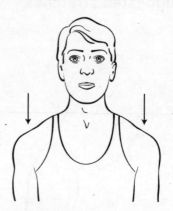

Push your shoulders down towards the floor.

Bring your shoulders forwards to meet each other at the front of the body.

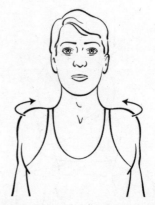

Pull your shoulders backwards to meet each other at the back of your body.

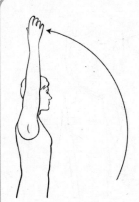

Lift your arms forwards
and up above your head.

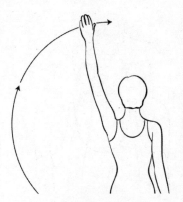

Lift your arms sideways
and up above your head.

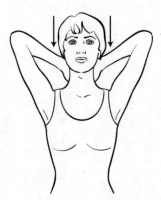

Place your hands on top of your
head and slide them down the back
of your head towards the floor.

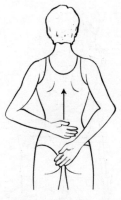

Place your hands on your
bottom and slide them up
towards your head.

With arms down by your side, bring your hands up to touch the front of your shoulders.

Let your hands slide down the front of your legs towards your feet.

Let your back slouch into a 'C' shape then sit upright again.

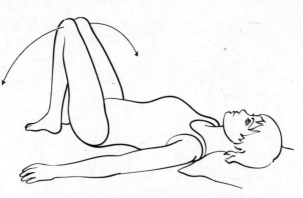

Keeping your knees together, let them roll from side to side. Keep your shoulders flat on the floor.

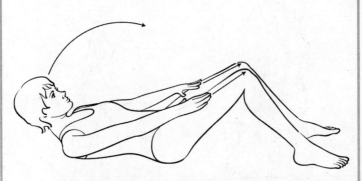

Place your hands on the front of your thighs and let them slide up towards the tops of your knees, keeping your chin tucked in.

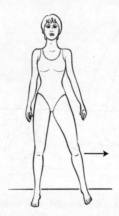

Take 3 steps to the left and then 3 steps to the right.

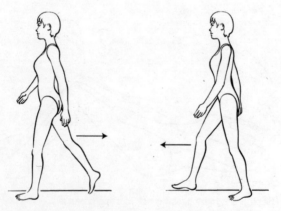

Take 3 steps backwards and then 3 steps forwards.

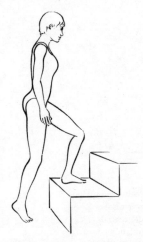

Face up a flight of stairs or a step. Step onto the lowest step, then bring the other foot up, onto the same step.

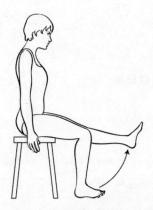

Straighten one leg out and return and repeat with the other leg.

Stand up from a sitting position trying not to use your hands to help.

Push downwards through your hands into the surface and then move up onto tip toes, as if looking over a high fence.

Index